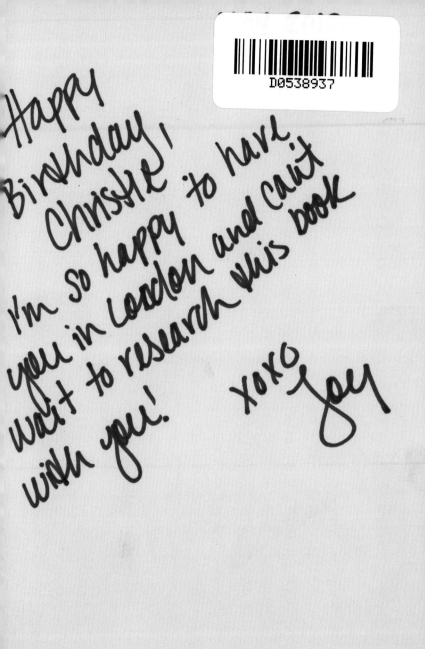

Happy
Birthday,
Christle,
I'm so happy to have
you in London and can't
wait to research this book
with you!

xoxo
Joy

Loch Ryan rock oysters packed shell down for transportation.

Colin Pressdee reviews over 150 restaurants, bars, markets, merchants, retailers and producers. Foreword by Charles Campion.

London
Oyster Guide

Shellfish
Association of Great Britain
in partnership with Graffeg

Contents

FOREWORD

Charles Campion

Charles Campion
Food writer and restaurant critic
www.charlescampion.com

I ate my first oyster in the spirit of curiosity and I don't remember having to summon up reserves of courage. Oysters may not be photogenic, indeed they look rather grey and quivery, but when you suck your first mollusc off the half shell you are rewarded with an elusive, minerally taste and an astonishing texture – softer than a politician's hand. I have always described oysters as tasting like a harbour at low tide and they certainly transport you to the seaside even when you're eating them in the heart of the big City.

> 'You are rewarded with an elusive, minerally taste and an astonishing texture'.

In the late 1990s when writing for the London Evening Standard I set my personal best for oysters. The idea was that I would go around town with a photographer in tow and have half-a-dozen oysters in as many different places as possible. We started at Billingsgate at 6.30 in the morning where we tried Duchy Natives with a pint of Guinness and that set the tone for the day. Oysters and pints were downed dutifully all morning, then through lunch and then afternoon tea, by the time we got to dinner we had slowed somewhat. At 8.30 pm the photographic record ceases abruptly, probably because I had to send the photographer home by taxi in some disarray. I enjoyed 87 oysters on that day and it is a record I am unlikely to better.

> 'I enjoyed 87 oysters on that day and it is a record I am unlikely to better'.

This would have been a very handy book to have had when I was planning my oyster mission. Colin Pressdee knows a thing or two about oysters, (indeed he's an expert on all kinds of seafood), and for him compiling this volume was a labour of love. In it you'll find over 150 of the best places to eat oysters in London, don't look for superficial wordy reviews or you'll be disappointed, but do expect all the relevant information in an elegant, easy to use format. This is a book written for oyster lovers by an oyster lover and will prove to be a handy memory-jogger when that craving for a dozen number twos sweeps over you.

It is also invaluable for anyone taking their first steps towards realising how very good oysters can be. I would urge anyone to stop when they scan a menu featuring bivalves and chose some oysters that they have never tried before. Fines de Claire supporters should try West Country Natives; Colchester Native diehards should try Scottish Rocks; if you like Belons try Irish Natives. That's the glory of oysters, they are all subtly different, and if a variety that is new to you doesn't ring your bell, you will still have capacity to follow them up with a dozen of your favourites.

> 'He was a brave man who first ate an oyster' so wrote Jonathan Swift.

Grumpy old Swift. Eating oysters doesn't call for bravery – an open mind, a love of good things and perhaps a splash of Tabasco is all you need to set the stage – plus a copy of this exceedingly useful little book!

INTRODUCTION

Colin Pressdee

Oysters through the ages

In their four hundred year occupation of Britain the Romans founded many oyster fisheries that supplied these delicacies back to Imperial Rome. It is said that the Emperor Tiberius lived on oysters most of his life; and indeed the advance of the Roman Legions could be traced by the mounds of oyster shells scattered across the country.

Through the ages oysters have been a delicacy. Who can forget the film of Fielding's 'Tom Jones' and the seductive scene eating oysters before another romantic night. Many millions of oysters were fished in the nineteenth century and by the mid twentieth century many of the fisheries had been depleted. The winter of 1962 – 3 virtually wiped out stocks in the shallower areas of the Colchester, Whitstable and Helford oyster beds.

In the early 1970s oyster cultivation became established with the faster growing Pacific oyster that had the advantage of not spawning in the colder British waters. Thirty years on there are now over twenty oyster farms and fisheries around the British coast. Though the industry is relatively small compared to that of France, the quality of British oysters is generally considered to be first class.

Despite the ups and downs in the fortunes of oyster fishing and farming the appreciation of oysters is evident from the increasing number of restaurants, particularly in London, that are selling oysters. Indeed there are many new oyster bars, gastro pubs and restaurants run by the modern era of chefs who appreciate the quality and provenance of British seasonal food, and the oyster plays an important part in their culinary repertoire.

The oyster is the most complete culinary experience. It has a unique flavour and texture that needs no accompaniment and no cooking. The juice and the meat of the oyster should be appreciated together. Half a dozen (or more) is a most satisfying meal at any time of the day. It delivers a bolt of protein and minerals that stimulates the system and invigorates the body.

The rock oyster is more elongated with a slightly crinkly shell, with a flat top shell and deep cupped bottom shell.

The native oyster is fairly round with a flat top shell and a cupped bottom shell.

Types of oysters
(p82-97)

There are two basic types of oyster eaten in Britain and Europe.

The native oyster (*ostrea edulis*) is indigenous and occurs naturally in many areas, particularly estuaries and shallow bays. The native oyster is known as edulis, flat, plat, and other names.

The Pacific oyster (*crassostrea gigas*) is reared in hatcheries (as are natives) and fed on algae until they are robust enough to be put into the sea. They are usually housed in mesh bags on trestles where they can grow by taking the natural nutrients from the sea. It is also called the gigas, rock oyster, deep oyster and cresuses.

For the purpose of this book, we shall call them rock oysters and native oysters, frequently qualified by their origin. There is a third type, the Portuguese oyster (*crassostrea angulata*), popular before the Pacific, but now rarely seen on the market.

The two types of oyster are easily recognisable. The Rock is more elongated with a slightly crinkly shell, with a flat top shell and deep cupped bottom shell. The native is fairly round with a flat top shell and a cupped bottom shell. There are many names for the different varieties of oysters, perhaps taken from the area such as Colchester, West Mersea, Whitstable, Loch Ryan, Helford, Loch Fyne and Cumbrae.

Oyster grades, purification, packing

Oysters are usually supplied graded and there are guidelines for the size by weight, although people handling oysters can judge a grade by appearance. In Britain natives were always graded as number one, two and three (plus four and five from some producers). Continental grades generally applied to rock oysters range from four zero (largest) to single zero down to number five. Largest average 300g each, the smallest are 30g each.

All oysters have to be purified by fully accredited systems before sale and each batch of oysters purified carries its own certification. Each oyster container carries a date of purification and a sell by / best before date.

Oysters will come from the fishery packed with the flat shell uppermost. This helps for the juice to be retained within the oyster should they open or gape slightly during transport. When storing oysters in a cool place or in the refrigerator always re-pack them the same way with the flat shells uppermost and cover them with a damp cloth.

Types of oysters

1. Jersey (r)
2. Menai (r)
3. Carlingford (r)
4. Loch Ryan (n)
5. West Mersea (r)
6. Colchester (r)
7. Poole (r)

Rock (r) Native (n)

Oyster seasons

The traditional season for natives was September 1 to April 30 or the winter months with an 'r'. The closed season was to allow them to spawn and come back into condition. They spawn in the warmer summer months and after spawning their body flesh takes a while to come back into good condition.

Rock oysters do not have a closed season, although they have now acclimatised to the British summer and many will be very ripe, over-plump and milky as though about to spawn. In some areas in a hot summer they have been known to spawn. Therefore over the summer many oyster aficionados take a rest from their favourite shellfish. Each fishery will monitor stocks and often stop supplying if the oysters become 'milky'.

Oyster fisheries and farms

Oysters are fished and farmed in over twenty locations around Britain. Notable beds are at Colchester, Maldon and Whitstable, and from the Solent to the Fal and the west coast of Scotland, Wales and Cornwall, and around the coast of Ireland.

The joy of oysters is that they vary from location to location in flavour and texture, with distinctive flavour notes just as tasting a wine. Each area has an individual nose, body and length of flavour, a mix of saltiness, sweetness, sapid and nutty nuances with vegetal and buttery tastes and textures.

Though many oyster lovers have their favourites all would sample ones from different areas eagerly, and many restaurants serve a variety of oysters from around the coast of Britain as well as some imported from France, particularly Fines de Claire from Brittany.

Opening oysters (p98-101)

Native and rock oysters are similar in that they have a flat top shell and a deep bottom one. They have a single hinge and one adductor muscle that holds the two shells together. The oysters can be opened either by breaking through the hinge and then slipping the knife to cut the adductor muscle; or the knife slipped in to the right hand side of the oyster to cut the adductor muscle first then the top shell removed, breaking the hinge.

In France nearly all oyster openers cut through the side to the muscle often with a very small, thin oyster knife. In Britain many openers use the hinge method. The side approach can cause tiny fragments of shell into the oyster whereas the hinge method can carry a speck of mud from the hinge. Both ways the oyster can easily be cleaned using the knife to remove any traces of mud or shell.

Larger native oysters are more difficult to open and the hinge needs to be broken first to enable a knife to penetrate to the muscle. A whole array of gadgets has been invented over the years to make opening easier, but used with care a simple oyster knife will suffice.

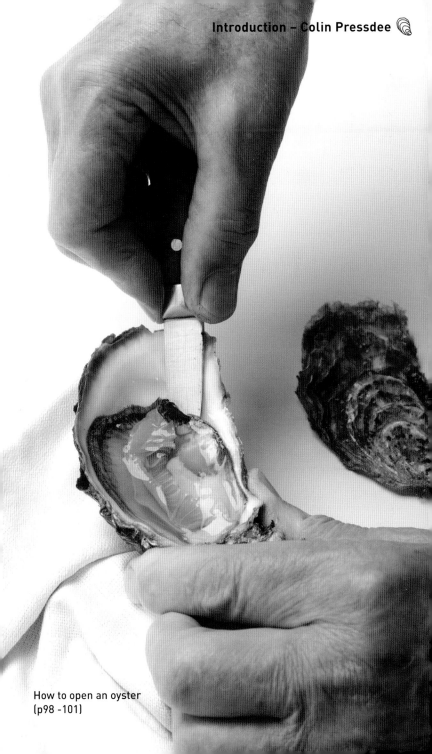

Introduction – Colin Pressdee

How to open an oyster
(p98 -101)

Experienced openers will use no protection for the hand, but it is recommended that the oyster is held steady on a board with a cloth so the knife does not slip and cause a cut.

I always open oysters on a tray to catch all the liquid from the shell. This liquid is not just sea water, but the oysters own juice that has a delicious flavour itself. There will be an excess of liquid which I always retain for use in a wide variety of recipes. The oysters should be presented in the deep shell with as much of the natural juice as possible.

Presenting oysters

Freshly opened oysters glisten in the light as a pearl glistens by day. The pure white of the shell with 'mother of pearl' highlights the soft cream colour of the oyster body and the dancing rays of the surrounding frill make an appetising presentation beyond compare, complete in every gastronomic aspect.

Such a pure food needs a simple but precise presentation and crushed ice is all that is required to set off the purity of the food. It also serves to keep the oysters cool that delivers them in perfection for appreciating their flavour and texture.

In France oysters are always presented with the adductor muscle attached to the bottom shell. The small flat oyster fork is used to cut the muscle then eat the oyster. In Britain generally the opener will cut the muscle cleanly from the deep shell so it can be slipped from the shell directly into the mouth.

I believe that an oyster should be chewed exactly as any meat or fish. The succulent flavour as the teeth sink into the firm and creamy flesh is an explosion of mineral nuances with the flavour of the seashore on the lowest spring tide. Merely to swallow an oyster misses this essential part of the oyster experience, but everyone to one's own.

'A loaf of bread' the Walrus said
'Is what we chiefly need:
Pepper and vinegar besides
Are very good indeed –
Now if you're ready, Oysters dear,
We can begin to feed.'

Alice in Wonderland, Lewis Carroll

• •

Accompaniments
(p103)

Purists might say that oysters require nothing in the way of sauces and accompaniments. Certainly the complete flavour of the oyster is remarkable and delicious in itself. A squeeze of lemon juice or vinegar just gives a touch of sharpness; a dash of Tabasco sauce certainly gives a kick that shellfish take so well; shallot vinegar brings an extra dimension, particularly to rock oysters; some like paprika, chilli vinegar, or even horseradish.

Caviar is probably the most natural partner to oysters. Half a teaspoon (or more) of caviar to crown an oyster makes a brilliant flavour combination. Other fish roe such as Avruga (from herring) or Keta (salmon) should not be overlooked as the flavour range is similar. Sea urchin (oursin) roe or coral is utterly delicious, delivering a deep iodine flavour that is a wow. The coral of lobster, particularly as the chef can cook the lobster keeping the coral inside its natural deep green raven-black colour, is truly wonderful to herald an oyster.

Oysters are so expressive they can take additional flavours well and it is fun trying some variations. Indeed at the purist restaurant Maison Prunier that was an institution in St James's, Madame Prunier also served her Oysters 'Variety Prunier' a plate of six, each one in different presentation.

• •

Cooking with oysters
(p104-127)

There are many who say cooking an oyster is heresy, but I have introduced numerous people to the gastronomic joys of oysters by giving them a cooked oyster. This introduces them to the unique elusive flavour of this regal mollusc, and soon they are tempted to try one 'au naturel'.

Most importantly, any cooked oyster dish should only involve frightening the oyster with heat rather than stewing it for a long time. A quick cooking process whether frying, grilling, baking or stewing just firms up the texture of the oyster without losing its wonderful flavour.

Oysters, as other molluscs such as mussels, cockles, and clams will take spice remarkably well. There are numerous other ingredients that will complement the flavour of oysters: spices, herbs, aromats, oils, sauces, butter, fungi, other shellfish such as oursins, dark crab meat, lobster coral, fish roe, caviar, vegetables, sea vegetables, cheese, wine, beer, sherry, citrus, vinegar, cured meat, and bacon are just some of the flavours that will make an exciting oyster experience.

Oysters bring a wonderful flavour to many dishes such as a steak and oyster pie, a seafood risotto, a soup, and such famous old specialities as 'carpetbag steak'.

The juice of the oyster should always be reserved for use in the oyster dish, and any excess juice

'The oyster has been eaten and appreciated in every country where civilisation has spread since eating ceased to be a mere necessity and became an art.'

Hector Bolitho in *The Glorious Oyster*.

Oyster with fried garlic, sesame and coriander. (recipe p120)

can be used to enhance any sauce, gravy, even a cocktail. Try adding oyster juice to a Bloody Mary! I will even freeze oyster juice in ice cubes for later use, but take care not to serve one in a gin and tonic. Yet oyster juice added to a glass of Muscadet or Gros Plant makes an invigorating drink.

I discovered this from an old French lady seated alongside us enjoying her lunchtime oysters in Terminus Nord in Paris. She tipped the excess juice from each of her dozen into a separate glass of Muscadet. On finishing her platter she picked up the glass and downed it in one. I would recommend it!

Drinks with oysters

Champagne, Chablis, Muscadet, Manzanilla: these wines have a propinquity with oysters for their dry, fresh, mineral, fruit and zesty character. Each in its way will enhance the flavour of the oyster and vice versa. I remember a somewhat acid Muscadet coming to life as I downed an oyster, and the flavour of the mollusc danced on my palate. The mineral character of Chablis matches the calcareous nature of the oyster as the chalky soil of Chablis and the shell of the oyster are a match together. The tiny bubbles of a chardonnay-based Champagne are akin to the effervescence in a breaking wave unleashing a host of dazzling flavours. The bodegas at Sanlucar de Barrameda where finest Manzanilla is matured are drenched with sea spray that brings the character of the ocean to the wine. Manzanilla, according to Javier Hidalgo, is the drink equivalent of an oyster, complete in character and perfect in style, flavour and length.

Many dry white wines complement oysters, and the picture broadens with cooked oyster dishes where the palette of flavours develops. Dishes such as Oysters Rockefeller, Kilpatrick or Mornay can be matched to wines with greatly varying depth and complexity.

In Ireland the obvious match for finest Galway or Cuan oysters is Guinness. The creamy smoothness and complex hop and malted nuances with a slightly bitter finish makes a great partner to oysters. Many other beers make a good match and also a dry cider is a pleasing combination.

It is hard to imagine a wine taster who does not appreciate oysters:

Javier Hidalgo of the renowned Sherry company in Sanlucar de Barrameda in Spain loves oysters.

'I drink La Gitana Manzanilla with oysters as it is the drink that reflects an oyster in its completeness. An oyster lacks nothing, neither does La Gitana.'

Charles Metcalfe, renowned wine 'obsessive' is a great oyster lover.

'It's important to have a fairly neutral wine that does not overpower with fragrances. Muscadet is a long time favourite as it comes alive with the saline flavour of the oyster. Picpoul de Pinet from the south of France has a delicious mineral complexity that picks up many of the subtle flavours of oysters. Similarly a dry Portuguese Vinho Verde from the arinto grape works well, as does an English Seyval Blanc. I adore the nutty sweetness of native oysters from Cornwall, Colchester or Ireland.
A drink to avoid in my opinion is Black Velvet, made from Guinness and Champagne. Indeed, how to take two great drinks and ruin both by mixing them. Separately they are delicious with oysters.'

17

London Oyster Guide

Where to dine out

A great friend and true oyster lover says she enjoys oysters at her leisure, whether standing at a bar or dining in a fine restaurant. Yet I know many who enjoy taking them on the hoof, and will stop and down half a dozen while walking through a market. In Borough Market Richard Haward's stand is usually surrounded with many oyster guzzlers; similarly in the Saturday market in Duke of York Square on Kings Road, or in Marylebone Market on Sundays, Maldon Oysters have their mobile oyster bar and enthusiasts keep a couple of openers busy all morning.

In the following pages there are over 150 places where oysters can be enjoyed. There are the London establishments that have served oysters for decades or centuries, and the new wave of oyster bars and restaurants that specialise in seafood. Many of the modern gastro bars make a feature of oysters, some even offering an oyster happy hour that's well worth seeking out. Some restaurants use oysters in novel ways in modern cuisine, and Japanese restaurants generally give some ingenious twists to flavour combinations in oyster shooters and other eastern dishes. Whether they are a main feature of a bar or restaurant, or make their mark in some remarkable dishes, I hope the following pages of entries will broaden the appeal and fascination of oysters for everyone.

Remember to check availability as some stick rigidly to the traditional season, whereas others might feature them on daily changing specialities. Whichever places you visit I do hope you will enjoy the glorious oyster in the following listings.

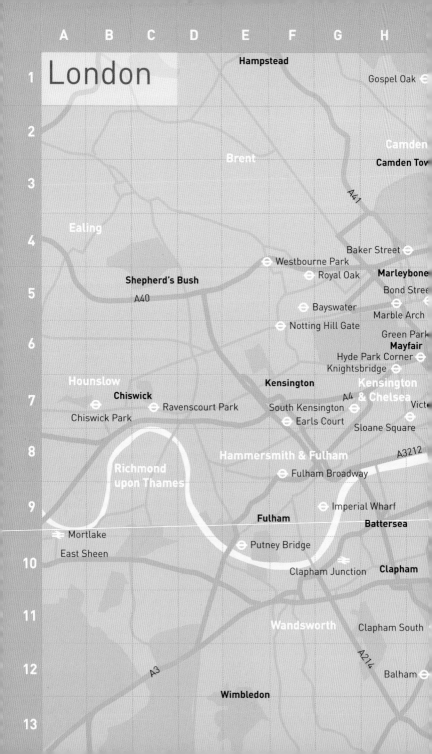

CENTRAL LONDON

Belgravia, Chelsea, Covent Garden, Fitzrovia, Green Park, Knightsbridge, Leicester Square, Marble Arch, Marylebone, Mayfair, Millbank, Notting Hill, Oxford Circus, Piccadilly, Soho, St James's, The Strand, Victoria, Westminster

Arbutus   Map J5

63 – 64 Frith Street, Soho,
W1D 3JW **020 7734 4545**
www.arbutusrestaurant.co.uk
⊖ Tottenham Court Road
Modern European

This extremely popular Soho restaurant changes its menu daily with seasonal market availability. Many ingenious combinations keep the menu exciting and alive including poached oysters with cucumber and salad burnett, and potato gazpacho with tartare of oysters and scallops. Wine from £16.50. 🎭 Theatre menu.

Back to Basics   Map J4

21a Foley Street, Marylebone,
W1W 6DS **020 7436 2181**
www.backtobasics.uk.com
⊖ Goodge Street / Oxford Circus
Neighbourhood restaurant

A simple neighbourhood restaurant with fresh seafood as the star in dishes that let natural flavours tell all. Rock – from £7.25. Wine from £16.95. Muscadet bargain of the guide. Al fresco.

Bank Westminster   Map J7

45 Buckingham Gate, Westminster,
SW1E 6BS **020 7630 6644**
www.bankrestaurants.com
⊖ St James's Park
Gastro bar brasserie

A mega bar and gastro restaurant that presents a host of seafood and brasserie dishes, including Carlingford Rocks, in a contemporary ambience. Rock – from £9.95. Wine from £15.95. Private room. Al fresco.

Bar Boulud   Map H6

Mandarin Oriental Hyde Park,
66 Knightsbridge, Knightsbridge,
SW1X 7LA
020 7201 3899
www.barboulud.com
⊖ Knightsbridge
New York brasserie

This smart brasserie from a renowned American chef is set in light airy rooms with pale elegant furnishings. A heavy French accent takes in charcuterie, Lyon saucisse, boudins, ris de veau, plus superb fish, seafood platter and rock oysters from Louth and Fines de Claire. Rock – from £12. Wine from £21.50. Private room. Accommodation.

Bellamy's

Map i5

18 – 18a Bruton Place, Mayfair,
W1J 6LY **020 7491 2727**
www.bellamysrestaurant.co.uk
⊖ Bond Street
Traditional French

This discreet and very French restaurant
sits well in the traditional Mayfair scene.
The bourgeois menu has many familiar
French dishes, Jersey Rock and Native
oysters. Rock and native – from £12. Wine
from £28.

Bentley's

Map J5

11 – 15 Swallow Street, Piccadilly,
W1B 4DG **020 7734 4756**
www.bentleys.org
⊖ Piccadilly Circus
Traditional oyster bar and restaurant

Oysters are a religion at this institution
that is switched on in its oyster selection.
Sample finest and freshest Maldon,
Scottish and Irish Rock, and Loch Ryan
Natives among a broad range. Rock and
native – from £9.50. Wine from £19.50.
Private room.

Bibendum

Map H7

Michelin House, 81 Fulham Road,
South Kensington, SW3 6RD
020 7581 5817
www.bibendum.co.uk
⊖ South Kensington
French / British

It wears its twenty-plus years well, both in
the elegant design and traditional/
contemporary style of cuisine that includes
plenty of seafood, and French and West
Mersea Native oysters. Native – from
£21.50. Wine from £19.95. Private room.

Bibendum Oyster Bar

Map H7

Michelin House, 81 Fulham Road,
South Kensington, SW3 6RD
020 7589 1480
www.bibendum.co.uk
⊖ South Kensington
French oyster bar

The basic style of this oyster and seafood
bar has a continental charm where the
freshest flavours of the sea shine. Enjoy
Fines de Claire Prestige, Colchester
Natives, West Mersea no.2, and Loch Ryan
oysters. Rock and native – from £10.75.
Wine from £19.95. Al fresco.

Bistro du Vin Soho

Map J5

36 Dean Street, Soho, W1D 4PS
020 7432 4800
www.bistroduvin.co.uk
⊖ Leicester Square
Modern bistro / brasserie

In the heart of theatre land, in Soho dining
here is artistry, theatre and showmanship
backed up by the amazing wine list and
selection by the glass. Sample Cornish
Natives and Rocks, or Fines de Claire and
finish with cheeses from the bespoke
cellar. Rock and native – from £15. Wine
from £18.50. Private Room. 🎭 Theatre
menu.

23

Bluebird Restaurant

Map G8

350 King's Road, Chelsea,
SW3 5UU **020 7559 1000**
www.bluebird-restaurant.co.uk
⊖ Sloane Square
Brasserie, café, bar

In another converted garage this Chelsea hub offers a café bar through to private fine dining with West Mersea Rocks. Rock – £10. Wine from £15. Private room. Al fresco.

Boheme Kitchen & Bar

Map J5

19 – 21 Old Compton Street, Soho,
W1D 5JJ **020 7734 5656**
www.bohemekitchen.co.uk
⊖ Leicester Square
European gastro bar

This contemporary European bar and restaurant in the heart of Soho bustles with fun and tasty food prepared at the open bar kitchen. Oysters feature regularly on the menu thoughout the season. Rock – from £12. Wine from £17.50. Al fresco. 🎭 Theatre menu.

Boisdale

Map i7

15 Eccleston Street, Belgravia,
W1W 9LX **020 7730 6922**
www.boisdale.co.uk
⊖ Victoria
Scottish

A wee tarry at this traditional restaurant in a Regency townhouse will find the joys of Loch Ryan Natives and Rossmore Rocks on the richly Scottish menu. Private members as well as public. Rock and native – from £9.75. Wine from £17.50. Private room or hire. Al fresco.

The Botanist

Map i7

7 Sloane Square, Sloane Square,
Chelsea, SW1W 8EE
020 7730 0077
www.thebotanistsloanesquare.com
⊖ Sloane Square
Contemporary gastro bar

This spacious elegant contemporary bar with flora imprinted in the design serves Rock and natives on its ingredient-driven menu at the bar or restaurant. Sample Maldon Rocks, Cumbrae Rocks and Duchy Natives from Wright Brothers. Rock and native – from £11. Wine from £16. 🎭 Theatre menu.

Brasserie St Jacques

Map J6

33 St James's Street, St James's,
SW1A 1HD **020 7839 1007**
www.brasseriestjacques.co.uk
⊖ Green Park
French brasserie

This Parisian brasserie in the heart of St James's serves finest rock oysters from Carlingford Lough. Rock – from £10.50. Wine from £16. Private room. Al fresco.

Brompton Bar & Grill

Map H7

243 Brompton Road, Knightsbridge,
SW3 2EP **020 7589 8005**
www.bromptonbarandgrill.com
⊖ South Kensington
Contemporary bistro

Another hub of the gastro scene in Knightsbridge, this contemporary and informal place features oysters on its menus at times throughout the season. Wine from £12. Private room.

The Cadogan Arms

Map G8

298 King's Road, Chelsea,
SW3 5UG **020 7352 6500**
www.thecadoganarmschelsea.com
⊖ Sloane Square or South Kensington
Gastro pub and dining

A traditional London pub with contemporary dining is a winning formula with Carlingford Rocks and traditional French wines on offer. Rock – from £13.50. Wine from £16, Muscadet £20.50. Private room.

Café Boheme

Map J5

13 Old Compton Street, Soho,
W1D 5JQ **020 7734 0623**
www.cafeboheme.co.uk
⊖ Leicester Square
French brasserie

Savour the fruits of the sea with Fines de Claire until the early hours in this authentic French style bar/brasserie in theatreland. Oysters feature regularly on the menu thoughout the season. Rock – from £11. Wine from £17.50, Muscadet £29.75, Picpoul de Pinet £27. Al fresco. Theatre menu.

Cambio de Tercio

Map F7

163 Old Brompton Road,
Kensington, SW5 0LJ
020 7244 8970
www.cambiodetercio.co.uk
⊖ South Kensington / Earls Court
Spanish tapas

This modern-style Spanish tapas bar serves a host of the mini dishes including vegetables, meat, charcuterie and seafood. Rock oysters, razor clams, mussels and gambas are just the thing with a copita or two of fine Hidalgo Manzanilla. Oysters – £17.50 (£2.95 each). Wine from £20.

Cape Town Fish Market

Map J5

5 – 6 Argyll Street, Oxford Circus,
W1F 7TE **020 7437 1143**
www.ctfm.com
⊖ Oxford Circus
Fish

This big, bustling seafood restaurant offers Cape salmon, kingklip and king fish with oysters completing the performance. Oysters – from £20.70 (£3.45 each). Wine from £16.95. Theatre menu.

Cave at Caviar House

Map J6

161 St James's Street, St James's,
W1V 9DF **020 7408 2900**
www.caviarhouse-prunier.com
⊖ Green Park
Luxury bar and restaurant

For a real taste of the best caviar, Balik smoked salmon, and oysters from perhaps Ireland, Cornwall, Essex and France, together with top Champagne, this is a fine destination. Oysters – from £16. Wine from £19.

Chabrot, Bistrot d'Amis

Map H6

9 Knightsbridge Green, Knightsbridge,
SW1X 7QL **020 7225 2238**
www.chabrot.co.uk
⊖ Knightsbridge
French bistro

A wonderful French ambience runs through both the small ground and first floor of this 'restaurant de coin' typical of any French town or city in its cuisine, wine and friendly atmosphere. Try Fines de Claire with sizzling chorizo. Oysters – from £9. Wine from £19.50.

Chez Patrick

Map F7

7 Stratford Road, Kensington,
W8 6RF **020 7937 6388**
www.chezpatrick.co.uk
⊖ Earls Court
French

This long-standing traditional restaurant serves truly French cuisine with plenty of seafood including Fines de Claire and Rossmore Natives in season in a relaxing ambience. Rock and native – from £10.90. Wine from £13.90. Muscadet £22.10.

The Commander

Map F5

47 Hereford Road, Notting Hill,
W2 5AH **020 7229 1503**
www.thecommanderbar.co.uk
⊖ Bayswater or Westbourne Park
Gastro bar

This modern gastro bar has an oyster counter displaying Carlingford, Maldon Rocks, and Duchy Natives from Wright Brothers. Oysters – from £1.80 each. Wine from £16, Muscadet £24, Picpoul de Pinet £23. Private Room. Al fresco.

The Cork & Bottle

Map J5

44 – 46 Cranbourn Street,
Leicester Square, WC2H 7AN
020 7734 7807
www.thecorkandbottle.co.uk
⊖ Leicester Square
Wine bar

This long-standing wine bar is in a cellar on Leicester Square. The food display counter shows glistening Irish Rock oysters, just the thing for a pre-theatre platter. Rock – from £12.95. Wine from £17.95. Al fresco. 😈 Theatre menu.

Corrigan's Mayfair

Map i5

28 Upper Grosvenor Street, Mayfair,
W1K 7EH **020 7499 9943**
www.corrigansmayfair.com
🚇 Bond Street
Modern British

This spacious restaurant with a great chef uses superb produce and amongst the finest pickings from the sea are rock and native oysters. Rock and native – from £12. Wine from £17.90 – 500ml carafe Picpoul de Pinet. Private Room.

The Cow

Map F5

89 Westbourne Park Road, Notting Hill,
W2 5QH **020 7221 0021**
www.thecowlondon.co.uk
🚇 Royal Oak
Traditional pub and dining

This traditional local pub is great for pint or bottle of wine with Irish or French oysters and terrific bar food. You can dine in the upstairs room on real British seasonal food. Rock – from £9.50. Wine from £15.75, Muscadet £26. Private hire. Al fresco.

The Ebury

Map i7

11 Pimlico Road, Chelsea,
SW1W 8NA **020 7730 6784**
www.theebury.co.uk
🚇 Sloane Square or Victoria
Gastro bar

This personification of a modern gastro bar has great style and a relaxed ambience with Colchester Rock oysters amongst its menu offerings. Rock – from £12. Wine from £16. Private room. 🎭 Theatre menu.

Electric Brasserie

Map E5

191 Portobello Road, Notting Hill,
W11 2ED **020 7908 9696**
www.electricbrasserie.com
🚇 Westbourne Grove
Bar brasserie

On the famous Portobello Road a bar leads to a sophisticated dark wood and mirrored brasserie serving an all day menu with steak tartare, crab soufflé, moules marinière and Fines de Claire.
Rock – from £13. Wine from £17.50, Muscadet £30. Private room. Al fresco.

Fishworks, Marylebone

Map i4

89 Marylebone High Street, Marylebone,
W1U 4QW **020 7935 9796**
www.fishworks.co.uk
🚇 Baker Street
Fish

A modern fishmonger with ethos, preparing the freshest, highest-quality fish attached to a restaurant where one can select the fish or crustacean from a wet fish display. Sample oysters from River Fal Natives, Maldon Rock and Colchester. Rock and native – from £10.50. Wine from £16.50, Muscadet £20.

Fishworks, Swallow Street

Map J5

7 – 9 Swallow Street, Piccadilly,
W1B 4DE **0207 734 5813**
www.fishworks.co.uk
⊖ Piccadilly Circus
Fish

This pristine modern fish bar and shop serves everything direct from the ice-filled counter. Spanking fresh fish and oysters from Cornwall, Maldon and Colchester. Rock and native – from £10.50. Wine from £16.50, Muscadet £20.

Geales, Chelsea Green

Map H7

1 Cale Street, Chelsea, SW3 3QT
020 7965 0555
www.geales.com
⊖ Sloane Square
Fish restaurant

A sister restaurant to the original with a similar style, where fresh seafood is the star of the show. Rock – from £10.50. Wine from £15.50, Picpoul de Pinet £22. Private room.

Geales, Notting Hill

Map F6

2 Farmer Street, Notting Hill
W8 7SN **020 7727 7528**
www.geales.com
⊖ Notting Hill
Fish restaurant

A traditional frontage with dark wood furniture and gingham tablecloths sets the scene for quality fish and Maldon oysters in truest style, with correct prices and service. Rock – from £10.50. Wine from £15.50, Picpoul de Pinet £22. Al fresco.

The Goring

Map i7

Beeston Place, Victoria, SW1W 0JW
020 7396 9000
www.thegoring.com
⊖ Victoria
Traditional British

The personification of British tradition and sophistication serves oysters when the 'r' is in the month. Rossmore oysters will then make an alternative to perhaps lobster omelette before the ever-popular beef wellington, on a very English menu. Oysters (on set menu). Wine from £27. Private Room. Al fresco. Accommodation.

The Grazing Goat

Map H5

6 New Quebec Street, Marylebone,
W1H 7RQ **020 7724 7243**
www.thegrazinggoat.co.uk
⊖ Marble Arch
Gastro pub and dining

This British country house pub and hotel in Central London is somewhere different for a plate of Carlingford Rock oysters. Rock – from £11.50. Wine from £18. Private room. Accommodation.

The Grazing Goat
Marylebone

Green's Restaurant & Oyster Bar

Map J6

36 Duke Street, St James's, SW1Y 6DF
020 7930 4566
www.greens.org.uk
⊖ Piccadilly Circus
Seafood restaurant

This traditional British seafood restaurant and oyster champagne bar serves finest West Mersea Rock and Wild Colchester Natives, and a great fishy menu. Rock and native – from £10.50. Wine from £19.50, Muscadet £24.50. Private room. Closed Sunday.

The Guinea Grill

Map i5

30 Bruton Place, Mayfair, W1J 6NL
020 7499 1210
www.theguinea.co.uk
⊖ Bond Street
British

This is a wonderful traditional food pub in Mayfair. A plate of Rossmore Natives or Rocks is just the thing before indulging in one of the best steaks in London. Rock and native – from £9.70. Wine from £19.95. Private room.

Harrods Food Hall Oyster Bar Caviar House-Prunier

Map H7

87 –135 Brompton Road, Knightsbridge,
W1X 7XL **020 7730 1234**
www.harrods.com
⊖ Knightsbridge
Food hall oyster bar

This legendary food hall with wonderful displays has an oyster bar at the end of the fish counter. Rocks and natives come from many sources. A great break from an indulgent shopping spree. Rock and native – from £12. Wine from £29.

Hawksmoor, Seven Dials

Map K5

11 Langley Street, Covent Garden,
WC2H 9JG **020 7856 2154**
www.thehawksmoor.co.uk
⊖ Covent Garden
British steak house

Appropriately set in a modern brewery in Covent Garden, come here to sample Cumbrae Rocks with Cumbrae sausages and a pint. A sister restaurant is situated in Combe's brewery in Covent Garden. Rock – from £12. Wine from £17, Picpoul de Pinet £19. Private room.

Hix at The Albemarle

Map J6

Brown's Hotel, Albemarle Street,
Mayfair, W1S 4BP **020 7518 4004**
www.thealbemarlerestaurant.com
⊖ Green Park
British

Located within Brown's Hotel, HIX at The Albemarle offers a truly glamorous, British dining experience. Marcus Verberne and Mark Hix have created an outstanding menu featuring carefully sourced ingredients. Choose from the a la carte menu, which also offers a traditional roast of the day from the trolley and regional dishes such as Fillet of Kingairloch red deer with new season Ardleigh vegetables. The perfect location for pre- or post-theatre meals, a set menu is also available.

The restaurant is also home to an amazing collection of British artists' work, including Tracey Emin, Rankin and Sue Webster. The room features wood-panelling,

elegant green banquettes and a small cocktail bar at which up to 4 guests may dine.

Rock and native – from £13.50. Brownsea Island Rocks, Duchy Cornwall Natives no.2. Wine from £20. Private room. 🎭 Theatre menu. Accommodation.

Hix Restaurant and Champagne Bar   Map i5

Selfridges, 400 Oxford Street,
Westminster, W1A 1AB
020 7499 5400
www.hixatselfridges.co.uk
Entrance via Duke Street
🚇 Bond Street
British and European

HIX Restaurant & Champagne Bar
overlooks the bustling accessory hall at
Selfridges. Located on the mezzanine
floor, it's the ideal spot to watch the
entertaining sport of 'handbag buying'.
Boasting a stunning pewter Champagne
and crustacean bar, the 90-seat restaurant
was designed by Conran. Mark Hix mixes
his signature British style food with some
classic European favourites – jacket potato
lobster thermidor is a winner, and the fish
fingers and chips is one of the biggest
selling dishes.

The Champagne Bar, showcasing small

independent Champagne producers, and
the artworks by British artists including
Tracey Emin, Mat Collishaw and Gary
Webb go towards making this the stores
most desirable stop-off for breakfast,
lunch, bar snax, afternoon tea and dinner.

Rock from £13.50. Cumbrae Rock oysters.
Wine from £20.

Hix   Map J5

66 –70 Brewer Street, Soho,
W1F 9UP **020 7292 3518**
www.hixsoho.co.uk
🚇 Piccadilly Circus
British

HIX Soho opened its doors to critical
acclaim in 2009 and soon after won
London's Time Out Award for Best New
Restaurant in 2010. The restaurant boasts
Mark Hix's signature daily-changing menu
of seasonal food, with such classics as
Heaven and Earth, and De Beauvoir
smoked salmon 'Hix cure'. With a
responsible attitude to sustainable fishing,
one can relax and enjoy the bounty of
seafood within the menu, amongst
beautifully prepared meat dishes.

Downstairs is the celebrated Mark's with
its apothecary bar and an eccentric
cocktail list designed by mixologist
extraordinaire Nick Strangeway, which go
hand in hand with Mark Hix's sumptuous
British bar snax. Try a Scotch quail's egg

with caper mayonnaise, or Welsh rabbit
fondue, washed down with a Hix Fix
cocktail.

Rock and native – from £13.50 Brownsea
Island Rocks, Brownsea Island with
Sillfield farm sausage, West Mersea Native
no.1. Wine from £20. Private room.
🎭 Theatre menu.

J Sheekey Oyster Bar

Map K5

28 – 34 St Martin's Court, Covent Garden,
WC2N 4AL **020 7240 2565**
www.jsheekeyoysterbar.co.uk
⊖ Leicester Square
Fish

This is possibly the most discreet venue in Covent Garden. The tranquil scene inside is the antithesis of the bustle outside. The art deco of the original J Sheekey, marble, mosaic and lacquered wood panels hung with photos of theatre luminaries carry a timeless ambience. Many come to appreciate this calm and enjoy the seafood specialities at their leisure.

The symmetrical 'U' shaped oyster bar has comfortable stools, the area softly lit by pearl dome lamps that make the bar glow. Here the finest West Mersea oysters, Maldons and Fines de Claire are enjoyed by many. But there are many other seafood specialities such as Dublin Bay prawns, razor clams, scallops, crab, lobster, tiger prawns and shrimps to be savoured or put together as a magnificent platter of fruits de mer.

The original J Sheekey restaurant that links with the newer oyster bar has a similar ambience of relaxed calm. The sweet scent of poached fish sings on the air as it has since first granted a licence

decades ago. The menu also takes in prime fish such as Dover and lemon sole, brill and salmon, with seasonal special dishes such as Esk sea trout with lovage and girolles, roast lobster with sweetbreads and salt baked bass. Old favourites include lobster thermidor and skate with nut brown butter and capers alongside pollack, haddock, bream and cod, not to mention the legendary fish pie.

The service is calm and considered even from the younger members of staff who fit into the mode with ease. The timeless feel is certainly something unique in London.

Rock and native – from £14.25.
Wine from £18.

J Sheekey

Map K5

28 – 34 St Martin's Court, Covent Garden,
WC2N 4AL **020 7240 2565**
www.j-sheekey.co.uk
⊖ Leicester Square
Fish

This renowned fish restaurant in the heart
of theatreland has very elegant and
comfortable dining with a wide selection of
fine fish and oysters including Dorset
Rocks, Strangford Lough, and West
Mersea Natives. Rock and native – from
£14.25. Wine from £21.75.

Kensington Place

Map F6

201 – 209 Kensington Church Street,
Kensington, W8 7LX
020 7727 3184
www.kensingtonplace-restaurant.co.uk
⊖ Notting Hill
European

London's first modern neighbourhood
brasserie is going strong with a daily-
changing menu that is strong on fresh fish,
and West Mersea Rocks come beautifully
presented. They are also available in their
fish shop next door. Oysters – £10.50.
Wine from £18.45. Private room.

Kettner's

Map J5

29 Romilly Street, Soho, W1D 5HP
020 7734 6112
www.kettners.com
⊖ Leicester Square
European

A Soho institution since 1867, the
restaurant has been gloriously revamped
and serves a variety of menus featuring
many classic French and European
specialities, including Maldon oysters.
Rock – from £12.50. Wine from £16.50.
Private room. 🎭 Theatre menu.

La Rueda, Kings Road

Map F9

642 King's Road, Chelsea,
SW6 2DP **020 7384 2684**
www.larueda-restaurant.com
⊖ Fulham Broadway
Spanish

A 'wheel' serves a full circle of hot and cold
tapas, including seafood, vegetarian and
meat dishes in traditional style with great
Spanish wines. Rock – from £7.50. Wine
from £12.95, Torres Vina Sol £15.50.
Private hire. Al fresco.

Le Boudin Blanc

Map i6

5 Trebeck Street, Shepherd's Market,
Mayfair, W1J 7LT **020 7499 3292**
www.boudinblanc.co.uk
⊖ Green Park
French

An authentic Parisian brasserie in the
heart of Mayfair's Shepherd Market that
bustles with Gallic charm where oysters
are obligatory on the menu. A great setting
for a 'plateau' of Jersey oysters.
Rock – from £8.70. Wine from £16.95.
Private room. Al fresco.

Le Café Anglais

Map F6

8 Porchester Gardens, Bayswater,
W2 4DB **020 7221 1415**
www.lecafeanglais.co.uk
⊖ Bayswater
Anglo French

This Anglo-French oyster bar and restaurant has the best seasonal produce and a wide selection at the bustling oyster bar. Choose from Maldon Rocks, Wild Blackwater Rocks, Prestige Fine de Claires, Kummamotos and Maldon Natives. Rock and native – from £8. Wine from £18. Private room.

Le Colombier

Map G7

145 Dovehouse Street, Chelsea,
SW3 6LB **020 7351 1155**
www.lecolombier-sw3.co.uk
⊖ South Kensington
French

This long-standing '*restaurant de quartier*' delivers French cuisine and ambience in the style of a Parisian brasserie with Fines de Claire and natives amongst its seafood selection. Rock and native – from £12. Wine from £18.50 – Chardonnay Vin Pays L'Aude. Private Room. Al fresco.

Le Suquet

Map H7

104 Draycott Avenue, Chelsea,
SW3 3AE **020 7581 1785**
⊖ South Kensington
Fish

This long-standing fish restaurant is noted for its platters of fruits de mer, plus a wide selection of fresh seasonal fish presented in classic French style. Fines de Claire and native oysters available in season. Oysters – from £13. Wine from £24.

Les Deux Salons

Map K6

40 – 42 William IV Street, Covent Garden,
WC2N 4DD **020 7420 2050**
www.lesdeuxsalons.co.uk
⊖ Charing Cross
Anglo French brasserie

This spacious traditional French brasserie could be on the Boulevard St Germain; the menu and setting has a real Gallic charm with true French specialities, and of course these include oysters. Finest plump Duchy Natives are on the regularly changing menu throughout the season. Native – from £13.95. Wine from £16.50, Muscadet £22. 🎭 Theatre menu.

L'Escargot

Map J5

48 Greek Street, Soho, W1D 4EF
020 7439 7474
www.lescargotrestaurant.co.uk
⊖ Leicester Square
Brasserie and restaurant

This long-standing Soho venue spread over several floors has some cutting-edge and traditional cuisine. Pristine rock oysters are among the starters. Rock – from £13.95. Wine from £19. Private room. Theatre menu.

Livebait, Covent Garden

Map K5

21 Wellington Street, Covent Garden, WC2E 7DN **0844 692 3900**
www.livebaitrestaurants.co.uk
⊖ Covent Garden
Fish

To experience the true beauty and simplicity of fresh fish and seafood, Livebait Covent Garden is a must. With an impressive bar at the entrance, once through the doors you won't be disappointed. The fabulous location provides a bustling yet intimate atmosphere, making it the perfect host from business lunches through to special evening meals.

Fish here is treated with respect in straightforward dishes that allow the natural flavours to shine through. Some of the fantastic dishes to sample include freshest rock oysters, classic moules marinières, traditional fish pie, queen scallop risotto, or grilled catch of the day.

Wines that elevate the freshness of the fish include Muscadet, Picpoul de Pinet and Albarino, or why not enjoy a pre-theatre glass of champagne and oysters at the bar.

Rock – from £9.50. Wine from £17, Muscadet £22. Theatre menu.

Loch Fyne

Map K5

2 – 4 Catherine Street, Covent Garden, WC2B 5JY **020 7240 4999**
www.lochfyne.com
⊖ Covent Garden
Seafood

The sister seafood restaurant has the same daily supplies of Loch Fyne Rocks. It's a perfect location for a platter pre or post-theatre. Rock – from £9.50. Wine from £12.95, Gros Plant £16.95. Private room. Theatre menu.

Massimo Restaurant & Oyster Bar — Map K6

Corinthia Hotel, Northumberland Avenue,
Westminster, SW1A 2BD
020 7998 0555
www.massimo-restaurant.co.uk
⊖ Embankment
Mediterranean seafood

Close to the River Thames, Trafalgar
Square, and the National Gallery this
restaurant and informal oyster bar serves
food all day. Rock species include Loch
Fyne, Speciales Perles Noires, Belon du
Belon 00. Rock – from £15. Wine from £25.
Private Room. 🎭 Theatre menu.

Mews of Mayfair — Map i5

10 Lancashire Court, New Bond Street,
Mayfair, W1S 1EY
020 7518 9388
www.mewsofmayfair.com
⊖ Bond Street
Modern European

Hidden down an alley off Bond Street, this
modern European restaurant has a
selection of Maldon oysters. Rock – from
£11. Wine from £16.50. Private room.
Al fresco.

Motcombs — Map i7

26 Motcomb Street, Belgravia,
SW1X 8JU **020 7235 6382**
www.motcombs.co.uk
⊖ Hyde Park Corner / Knightsbridge
Modern British

A Belgravia institution serving natives and
rocks opened in front of eager oyster
lovers in the bar. Dining extends into a
brasserie and downstairs restaurant.
Rock and native – from £9. Wine from
£16.85, Chateau Tour Sauvignon Blanc
£20.85. Private room. Al fresco.

Nobu Berkeley Street — Map i6

15 Berkeley Street, Mayfair,
W1J 8DY **020 7290 9222**
www.noburestaurants.com
⊖ Green Park
Japanese

Innovative stylish international Japanese
cuisine including rock oysters with a range
of racy sauces and new style sashimi.
Rock – from £18 with choice of sauces.
Wine from £29. Private room.

Nobu London — Map i6

Metropolitan Hotel, 19 Old Park Lane,
Mayfair, W1K 1LB
020 7447 4747
www.noburestaurants.com
⊖ Hyde Park Corner
Japanese

This elegant restaurant overlooking Hyde
Park serves the finest oysters alongside
sushi from the master of contemporary
Japanese cuisine. New style sashimi and
dazzling oysters with racy sauces reach
taste buds unknown to other cuisines.
Rock – from £18. Wine from £29. Private
room. Accommodation.

One-O-One

Map H6

Sheraton Park Tower, 101 Knightsbridge,
Knightsbridge, SW1X 7RN
020 7290 7101
www.oneoonerestaurant.com
◉ Knightsbridge
Seafood

Sophisticated Breton-inspired seafood
dishes are competently executed,
including a choice of three oysters
prepared in novel styles or fresh with
shallot vinegar. Oysters – £17. Wine from
£22. Private room. Accommodation.

The Orange

Map i7

37 Pimlico Road, Victoria, SW1W 8NE
020 7881 9844
www.theorange.co.uk
◉ Sloane Square
Gastro pub and dining

The sleek design of this gastro bar is in
keeping with the Cubit lines. Stylish bar
and restaurant menus include Carlingford
Lough Rocks. Rock – from £11.50. Wine
from £16. Private room. Al fresco.

The Pantechnicon

Map i6

10 Motcomb Street, Belgravia,
SW1X 8LA **020 7730 6074**
www.thepantechnicon.com
◉ Hyde Park / Knightsbridge
Gastro pub and dining

Another of Cubitt's sophisticated gastro
pubs that bustles with well-heeled locals
enjoying Colchester Rocks. A country
house style first floor restaurant is for
relaxed dining. Rock – from £11.50.
Wine from £18. Al fresco.

Pescatori, Fitzrovia

Map J5

57 Charlotte Street, Fitzrovia,
W1T 4PD **020 7580 3289**
www.pescatori.co.uk
◉ Goodge Street
Italian seafood

This popular Italian seafood restaurant has
a daily specials board for the freshest fish
from the market including rock oysters.
Oysters – £10.95. Wine from £18.50.
Private room. Al fresco. Closed Sunday.

Pescatori, Mayfair

Map i6

11 Dover Street, Mayfair, W1S 4LH
020 7493 2652
www.pescatori.co.uk
◉ Green Park
Italian seafood

A wide range of fresh fish comes in a
variety of tasty presentations, either from
the grill or oven with a delicate use of
herbs and sauces. Rock oysters are served
au naturel. Rock – from £10.95. Wine from
£18.50. Private room. Closed Sunday.

The Pig's Ear

Map G8

35 Old Church Street, Chelsea,
SW3 5BS **020 7352 2908**
www.thepigsear.info
⊖ South Kensington
Gastro pub and dining

This large Chelsea pub has been
sympathetically made over, particularly
with its traditional cuisine from prime
British ingredients including rock oysters
from Strangford Lough. Rock – from £11.
Wine from £14.95. Private hire.

Poissonnerie de l' Avenue

Map H7

82 Sloane Avenue, Chelsea, SW3 3DZ
020 7589 2457
www.poissonneriedelavenue.com
⊖ South Kensington
Fish

This long-standing fish restaurant and fish
shop still serves the freshest oysters
including Loch Ryan Wild no.2, West
Mersea no.2, and Whistable no.1, 2 and 3
from behind the bar. The menu includes
many old favourite, almost forgotten,
traditional seafood dishes and sound
grilled and poached fish. Rock and native
– from £7.50. Wine from £26 – Sauvignon
Haut Poitou. Private room.

Quaglino's

Map J6

16 Bury Street, St James's, SW1Y 6AJ
020 7930 6767
www.quaglinos-restaurant.co.uk
⊖ Green Park
Anglo French brasserie

An elegant sweeping staircase leads to the
spacious, airy dining room with a large
fruits de mer bar displaying Maldon
oysters as a backdrop. Rock and native –
from £12.50. Wine from £19, Muscadet
£27.50. Private room. Closed Sunday.

Quilon

Map J7

41 Buckingham Gate, Westminster,
SW1E 6AF **020 7821 1899**
www.quilon.co.uk
⊖ St James's Park
West Coastal Indian cuisine

Oysters, as other molluscs, take spice well
to complement the subtle flavours. Here
try spiced stir-fried oysters, rock oysters
crusted with lentil and spices served with
onion relish amongst other notable
creations. Rock – from £15. Wine from
£20. Al fresco. Private room.

Quo Vadis

Map J5

26 – 29 Dean Street, Soho, W1D 3LL
020 7437 9585
www.quovadissoho.co.uk
⊖ Leicester Square
Modern British

This revamped long-standing and ever popular Soho restaurant serves exceedingly fine dishes from well-sourced British ingredients. Commendably unfussy cuisine, and great Cumbrae oysters. Oyster happy hour is a bargain.
Rock – from £13.80. Wine from £18.
Private room. Al fresco. 🎭 Theatre menu.

Racine

Map H7

239 Brompton Road, Knightsbridge, SW3 2EP **020 7584 4477**
www.racine-restaurant.com
⊖ Knightsbridge
French

This 'homage to traditional French food' serves exciting dishes across a broad range of styles, from simply the freshest seafood, including Dorset Brownsea rock oysters, to complex culinary creations.
Rock – from £14.50. Wine from £20, Picpoul de Pinet £21. Private room.

Racine
Knightsbridge

Randall & Aubin

Map J5

16 Brewer Street, Soho, W1F 0SQ
020 7287 4447
www.randallandaubin.com
⊖ Piccadilly Circus
Seafood

In bustling Brewer Street Soho Randall and Aubin is one of London's landmark oyster bars. A former butcher's shop key elements of the original décor have been retained and the white tiled walls and marble topped tables create a wonderful, unique dining atmosphere with subtle clues to the past. A bountiful seafood counter packed with fresh produce tempts you on arrival – oysters, lobsters, prawns, mussels, whelks, crabs, langoustines and clams. Savour a platter of the fruits de mer or if this is too much try a smaller 'assiette'. The menu extends to a full carte with crab cakes, queen scallops, calamaris, gravadlax, moules and tuna nicoise amongst the starters. Mains range from fish and chips to grilled sea bass, or a seafood grill. Meat from the rotisserie includes belly pork, Loire chicken, roast salt beef and loin of lamb. For a quick snack there are eggs Benedict, chicken Caesar and substantial baguettes. Oysters come in their season: plump natives, Fines de Claire and rocks, or cooked as oysters Kilpatrick. Oyster Happy Hour (3 – 6pm) and is a bargain. Enthusiastic young staff keep service on the ball and the place buzzing. It's a great place to unwind, listen to modern music, and watch the Soho world go by.

Rock and native – from £8.85. Special 6 rock oysters and glass of Champagne Monday–Friday 3pm – 6pm. Rock oysters, Fine de Claire, native, Oyster Kilpatrick, Oyster of the month. Wine from £16.95.

Rex Whistler Restaurant at Tate Britain

Map K7

Tate Britain, Millbank, Westminster,
SW1P 4RG **020 7887 8225**
www.tate.org.uk
⊖ Pimlico
Modern British

There are few restaurants with original hand-painted murals by a renowned Victorian artist. The airy elegant room is well known for prime British food and its fabulous wine list at amazing prices. Enjoy Colchester Rocks with a glass of Chablis or Champagne before a prime organic lamb loin, slow cooked belly pork, or steak pie. Rock – from £15.60. Wine from £15.50. Open lunchtimes only.

Roux At The Landau

Map J5

The Langham, Portland Place,
Marylebone, W1B 1JA
020 7965 0165
www.thelandau.com
⊖ Oxford Circus
French

This light airy room with Romanesque windows and soft pastel colours is the setting for some of the finest classic French cuisine in London. The seasonal use of ingredients is impressive, including oysters served in their traditional months. Oysters – from £22. Wine from £29. Private room. Accommodation.

Rules

Map K6

35 Maiden Lane, Covent Garden,
WC2E 7LB **020 7836 5314**
www.rules.co.uk
⊖ Covent Garden
Traditional British

This London institution since 1798 is a bastion of tradional British food. Seafood, meat and game excels as do Wild Cumbrae, Brownsea Island Dorset Rocks, Duchy Natives. Rock and native – from £12. Wine from £22.50. Private room.

The Savoy Grill

Map K5

The Savoy, The Strand, WC2R 0EU
020 7592 1600
www.gordonramsay.com/thesavoygrill
⊖ Charing Cross
British

The sumptuous décor of the new Savoy is the setting for some of the finest classic British and French cuisine with silky service featuring Cumbrae rock oysters on a fabulous menu. Rock – from £10.50. Wine from £22 – Cotes de Gascoigne. Private room. 🎭 Theatre menu. Accommodation.

Scott's

20 Mount Street, Mayfair, W1K 2HE
020 7495 7309
www.scotts-restaurant.com
⊖ Green Park
British

One of Mayfair's most renowned seafood restaurants was reborn several years ago to greater style. Dine around the central oyster bar on freshest seafood and British meat. Sample Fine de Claires, Strangford Loughs, West Mersea no.2, Dorset Rocks. Rock and native – from £11.25. Wine from £24 – Marsanne-Viognier. Private room. Al fresco.

Seaport

24 Seymour Place, Marble Arch, W1H 7NL **020 7724 5001**
www.seaportrestaurant.co.uk
⊖ Marble Arch
Italian / Pacific

This unpretentious popular Mediterranean restaurant relies on quality seafood and simple Italian / Pacific cooking to deliver 'beach style' fish dishes. The seafood platter, clams, langoustines and rock oysters are great favourites. Rock – from £9. Wine from £14.

Selfridges Champagne & Oyster Bar

400 Oxford Street, Westminster, W1A 1AB
0800 123400
www.selfridges.com
⊖ Bond Street
Oysters and caviar

Located in the food hall with seats around, a bar with seafood and Caviar, Jersey rocks, West Mersea Rocks, Cumbrae, Prestige, and Native Loch Ryan. Rock and native – from £11.30. Wine from £25.60 – Selfridges Chablis.

Simpson's-in-the-Strand

100 Strand,The Strand, WC2R 0EW
020 7836 9112
www.simpsonsinthestrand.co.uk
⊖ Charing Cross
British

This bastion of Britishness is famous for its roasts from the trolley. A plate of natives makes a great start to a traditional meal. Native – from £18.50. Wine from £27.75 – Pinot Grigio. Private room. 🎭 Theatre menu.

St John Hotel

Map J5

1 Leicester Street, Soho, WC2H 7BL
020 3301 8069
www.stjohnhotellondon.com
⊖ Leicester Square
British

The original Manzi's fish restaurant and hotel newly opened under the St John banner could not have a better team to recreate the classic seafood and British dishes. Huitres, langouste, and moules are served in the classic dining room with first class service and wines. Native – from £15. Wine from £26. 🎭 Theatre menu. Accommodation.

Terroirs

Map K6

5 William IV Street, Covent Garden, WC2N 4DW **020 7036 0660**
www.terroirswinebar.com
⊖ Charing Cross
French wine bar and bistro

This French wine bar with traditional character specialises in charcuterie and artisan products, with Maldon Rocks completing a pleasing package with wonderful regional wines. Rock – from £10.80. Wine from £16.50, Sauvignon de Touraine £18.50. Closed Sunday.

The Thomas Cubitt

Map i7

44 Elizabeth Street, Belgravia, SW1W 9PA
020 7730 6060
www.thethomascubitt.co.uk
⊖ Victoria
Gastro bar and dining

Named after the renowned Victorian master builder, this modern bustling gastro pub (now a group) downstairs with an elegant upstairs dining area; oysters can be enjoyed in both with Carlingford Rocks served with shallot vinegar. Rock – from £11.50. Wine from £20. Private room. Al fresco.

Tsunami

Map J4

93 Charlotte Street, Fitzrovia, W1T 4PY **020 7637 0050**
www.tsunamirestaurant.co.uk
⊖ Goodge Street
Japanese

Try the rock oysters served as 'sunkiss seafood' served in hot olive oil drizzled with ponzu, or oyster shooters with sake, ponzu, momiji oroshi, quail egg and scallion. Oysters – from £12.50. Wine from £16.50.

The Toucan

Map J5

19 Carlisle Street, Soho, W1D 3BY
020 7437 4123
⊖ Tottenham Court
Pub

A Guinness-themed pub with the Toucan proudly displayed is where a pint and a few Rossmore oysters can be enjoyed all afternoon. Oysters £5 – a bargain of the guide. Wine £13.50.

Wright Brothers Soho Oyster House

Map J5

13 Kingly Street, Soho, W1B 5PW
020 7434 3611
www.wrightbrotherssoho.com
⊖ Oxford Circus
Seafood

Close to Carnaby Street, still swinging since the swinging sixties, is the discreet façade of the new Soho oyster bar. It runs through into a small gastro yard where several restaurants share the al fresco area. The split levels make for interesting casual eating, for either a plate of smoked salmon, or a full feast of oysters and seafood washed down with a glass of the mainly French wines on the list. There is plenty of ale, porter, stout, aperitifs and Manzanilla to choose from. The mezzanine is perhaps for more comfortable dining, while the bar at the al fresco level is for a casual glass or snack. Down again is a traditional oyster bar with high tables and plenty of bar seating. Diners can pick and mix a fruits de mer from langoustines prawns, winkles, whelks, mussels, clams and crab then adorn it with a bed of three oysters from the Wright Brothers own Duchy Oyster Farm or Brownsea Island, Carlingford, Cumbrae or Speciales de Claire. Other house specials include Cornish crab, fish pie, and ox cheek, ale and oyster pie. There are several specials every day on a Prices chalkboard, perhaps home-made fish cakes or slow-cooked belly pork with scallops. At the bar the hot oyster dishes are chalked up, perhaps oysters Rockefeller, Kilpatrick or Mornay. Die-hards will want to devour the oysters au naturel with some brown bread or there's the traditional shallot vinegar, lemon juice or Tabasco sauce to keep numerous regulars extremely happy.

Rock and native – from £6.50. Rock oysters, Duchy natives, Colchester, Maldon, Spéciale de Claire, Carlingford. Wine from £20.

Wheeler's of St James's

Map i6

72 St James's Street, St James's,
SW1A 1PH **020 7408 1440**
www.wheelersrestaurant.org
⊖ Green Park
Fish

Close to the site where Madame Prunier
held court, the legendary name of
Wheeler's has been recreated and the
style ingeniously brought into the 21st
century. Hors d'oeuvres, seafood cocktails,
Dover sole, and halibut all feature with
oysters understated, yet served as a
Boston-style oyster cocktail or rocks au
naturel. Rock – from £10.50. Wine from
£19. Private room.

Wholefoods Market – The Merchant of Vino

Map F6

63-79 Kensington High Street,
W8 5SE **929 7368 4514**
www.wholefoodsmarket.co.uk
⊖ High Street Kensington

This bar on the first floor grazing area
serves Maldon and Colchester rock oysters,
with a fair selection of wines; enjoy at the
bar or the intimate seating area. Oysters
£5.95 (99p each). Wine from £15.99.

Wiltons

Map J6

55 Jermyn Street, St James's,
SW1Y 6LX **020 7629 9955**
www.wiltons.co.uk
⊖ Green Park
British

This institution, since 1742, is where the
legendary maître Jimmy Marks ruled for
decades, into his nineties. Renowned for
its finest Colchester oysters, baby lobster,
langoustines, Dover sole and wild Scottish
salmon, the ambience is the
personification of true British catering.
Oysters – from £12. Wine from £30. Private
room. Closed Saturday and Sunday.

The Wolseley

Map J6

160 Piccadilly, Mayfair, W1J 9EB
020 7499 6996
www.thewolseley.com
⊖ Green Park
Modern European

This 'Grand Café' in European style serves
its all day menu of finest British and
European cuisine to a very discerning
clientele. Enjoy the Fines de Claire
Prestige and Cumbrae Rocks and perhaps
a tankard of Black Velvet. Rock – from £12.
Wine from £19.50.

Zilli Fish

Map J5

36 – 40 Brewer Street, Soho,
W1F 9TB **020 7734 8649**
www.zillirestaurants.co.uk
⊖ Piccadilly Circus
Fish

This modern seafood restaurant with
stylish décor is the setting for seafood
cuisine and tasty Jersey rock oysters.
Rock – from £8.10. Wine from £19.50.
Private room. Closed Sunday.

Finchley, Hampstead, Islington, Kings Cross, London Fields

The Brasserie on St John Street

Map L3

360 – 362 St John Street, Islington,
EC1V 4NR **020 7837 1199**
www.the-brasserie.com
⊖ Angel
Fish brasserie / bar

Just south of the bustling Upper Street this modern fish restaurant and bar broadens the area's choice and is a great stop off before an evening at Sadler's Wells.
Rock – from £11.10. Wine from £14.50.
Private room. 🎭 Theatre menu.

The Bull and Last

Map i1

168 Highgate Road, Hampstead,
NW5 1QS **020 7267 3641**
www.thebullandlast.co.uk
⊖ Gospel Oak
Gastro bar and dining

This historic grade two pub near Hampstead Heath has been given a new lease of life by a forward-thinking team. Oysters are served at the bar and in the restaurant. Rock – from £11.10 or £1.85 each at the bar. Wine from £15, Picpoul de Pinet £22. Al fresco.

Fish Central

Map M4

149 – 155 Central Street, Islington,
EC1V 8AP **020 7253 4970**
www.fishcentral.co.uk
⊖ Old Street
Modern fish and chips

This modern fish and chip shop is beautifully designed with soft pastel décor and furniture, a natural fishing theme and a menu that elevates this traditional food. Sample West Mersea Rock, Scottish and Irish natives and oysters au gratin.
Rock and native – from £7.50. Wine £11.95.
Private room. Al fresco.

The Prince Arthur

Map O2

95 Forest Road, London Fields,
E8 3BH **020 7249 9996**
www.theprincearthurlondonfields.com
⊖ Bethnal Green
Gastro pub and dining

Re-established as a real gastro pub with dining, it serves many homely traditional bar food dishes in a comfortable pub ambience. Sample the Duchy native oysters from Wright Brothers, Borough Market. Native – from £14.50. Wine from £16, Sauvignon Haut Poitou £22.
Private hire.

Smithy's

Map K3

The Stables, 15 –17 Leeke Street,
Kings Cross, WC1X 9HY **020 7278 5949**
www.smithyslondon.com
Ⓣ Kings Cross St Pancras
Modern British

Smithy's is set in old stables, originally
housing the shire horses that pulled the
London Street omnibuses. The British and
European menu includes fresh rock
oysters. Rock – from £9.50. Wine from
£17.50 – Sauvignon Casa Azur. Private hire.

The St Pancras Grand and Champagne Bar

Map K4

Upper Concourse, St Pancras Station,
St Pancras, N1C 4QL
020 7870 9900
www.stpancrasgrand.co.uk
Ⓣ Kings Cross St Pancras
Oyster bar and restaurant

Opposite the longest champagne bar in
Europe, overlooking the Eurostar terminal,
is the destination brasserie. Enjoy
Carlingford Lough, Dorset Rock, Maldon,
Jersey, Duchy and Wild Loch Ryan Natives.
Perhaps 6 rock oysters and glass of
Muscadet? Rock and native – from £12
Wine from £26.50. Private room. Al fresco.

Two Brothers Fish

297 – 303 Regent's Park Road, Finchley,
N3 1DP **020 8346 0469**
www.twobrothers.co.uk
Ⓣ Finchley Central
Fish and Chip Shop

This upmarket fish and chip shop serves
everything from sardines to Dover sole,
crisp-fried in matzo meal, steamed or
grilled. Rock – from £8.95. Wine from
£14.50.

The Prince Arthur
London Fields

Bethnal Green, Canary Wharf, City of London, Clerkenwell, Docklands, Farringdon, Greenwich, Shoreditch, Spitalfields

1 Lombard Street Brasserie   Map M5

1 Lombard Street, City of London,
EC3V 9AA **020 7929 6611**
www.1lombardstreet.com
⊖ Bank
European

A great bar / brasserie and fine dining restaurant in the heart of the City, serving consistently fine meat and fresh seafood. Oysters are served mainly during the traditional season at the bar and in the brasserie. Rock and native – from £12. Wine from £21. Private room. Closed Sunday.

Bistro du Vin & Bar, Clerkenwell   Map L4

40 St John Street, Clerkenwell, EC1M 4DL
020 7490 9230
www.bistroduvinandbar.com
⊖ Farringdon
Modern bistro / brasserie

The concept of Bistro du Vin has arrived in London. Its modern sophistication is that of dining in informality, with a motto of 'I think. Therefore I du Vin.' The amazing wine list is backed up with oysters, moules, lobster, steak and coq au vin. Rock and native – from £15. Wine from £18.50. Private Room.

Boisdale of Bishopsgate   Map N5

Swedeland Court, 202 Bishopsgate,
Bishopgate, EC2M 4NR
020 7283 1763
www.boisdale.co.uk/bishopsgate
⊖ Liverpool Street Station
Scottish

From the highlands and the lowlands, the isles and lochs, this traditional gentlemans' oyster bar in the City has some of Scotland's finest including Loch Ryan Natives, Jersey and Colchester Rocks. Rock and native – from £6.30. Wine from £17.50, Muscadet £25.00. Private room. Closed Saturday and Sunday.

Boisdale of Canary Wharf   Map R6

Cabot Place, Canary Wharf, E14 4QT
020 7715 5818
www.boisdale.co.uk/canary-wharf
⊖ Canary Wharf
Scottish

With its views of the City skyline, oyster lovers will find this a great refuge in the financial quarter, where the natural flavours of the ocean are such a contrast to a regimented office. Rock and native – from £9.75. Wine from £17.50. Private room. Closed Sunday.

The Boundary

2 – 4 Boundary Street, Entrance on
Redchurch Street, Shoreditch, E2 7DD
020 7729 1051
www.theboundary.co.uk
⊖ Liverpool Street
French brasserie and fruits de mer

This recently converted impressive
Victorian warehouse is in the new trendy
area of Shoreditch. The conversion has
discreetly imposed elegant modern design
in the three restaurants, bars and the
twelve bespoke bedrooms and five suites.
The roof restaurant and bar with al fresco
area has wonderful vistas of the London
skyline. The love of Parisian brasseries
comes through in impressive fruits de
mer, and a host of seasonal produce that
includes gulls eggs, asparagus, grouse,
game, wild berries and funghi as the
culinary calendar unfolds. In the open
kitchen chefs beaver producing platters of
oysters from fisheries of Scotland and
England, Cornish lobster and crab, Dover
sole and line caught seasonal fish taking in
skate, monk, halibut, sole and bass. The
fruits de mer comes in one, two or three
tiers adorned with lobster, grises,
langoustines, prawns, clams, oysters,
cockles and mussels. Escargots
bourguignonne, confit de canard, veal
brains in caper butter, beef fillet with bone

marrow and snails, English veal, Landes
chicken, haunch of venison and suckling
pig roast are among the salivating offers
for meat lovers. The impressive wine list
takes in the finest of Europe yet starts with
house wine in carafes and under £20 a
bottle with sixty wines under £35 a bottle
with over 500 Prices bins in total. Prix fixe
menus make this affordable for a broad
range of people who can relax and enjoy
the fabulous surroundings and the correct
discreet amiable service.

Rock and native – from £12. Rocks from
Scotland and England, Rockefeller oysters.
Wine from £18. Private room.
Accommodation. Basement level – large
seafood selection.

Brawn

Map N4

49 Columbia Road, Bethnal Green,
E2 7RG **020 7729 5692**
www.brawn.co/
⊖ Hoxton
French wine bistro

The wide menu of country food takes in charcuterie, taste ticklers of Maldon oysters, anchoïade, and Basque saucisse. Shetland mussels, Cornish crab, pigs' trotters and tête de veau are amongst tempting dishes. As with its sister Terroirs, discover the best of French regional wines. Rock – from £10.80. Wine from £14.50, Muscadet £22.25.

Catch

Map N5

Andaz Hotel, 40 Liverpool Street,
EC2M 7QN **020 7618 7200**
www.andazdining.com
⊖ Liverpool Street
Seafood

This modern restaurant with a crustacean bar displays a selection of the freshest seafood including Irish Mourny Rock, Maldon, Blackwater, and Kumomoto. Rock and native – from £12. Wine from £20. Private room. Accommodation.

Chamberlain's

Map N5

23 – 25 Leadenhall Market, City of London,
EC3V 1LR **020 7648 8690**
www.chamberlains.org
⊖ Bank
Fish

This elegant traditional restaurant is situated in the heart of the City in Leadenhall Market, providing a unique Victorian elegance for a plate of Irish rocks. Rock – from £14.50. Wine from £21.50. Private room. Al fresco

Coq d'Argent

Map M5

1 Poultry, City of London, EC2R 8EJ
020 7395 5000
www.coqdargent.co.uk
⊖ Bank
Grand brasserie

Located high over the City, this sleek restaurant has a beautiful roof garden with breathtaking views of St Paul's Cathedral and the City of London. It's a fine setting for a platter of Colchester rock oysters. Oysters – from £11.25. Wine from £19.75. Private room. Al fresco.

The Empress of India

Map P3

130 Lauriston Road, Victoria Park,
E9 7LH **020 8533 5123**
www.theempressofindia.com
⊖ Mile End
Classy Gastro pub

The Indian theme of the mirrors and murals gives a colonial feel for some very decent gastro bar food. Try dressed crab, prawns mayonnaise, Duchy Natives, herb crusted hake and game pie.
Native – from £14.50. Wine from £16, Muscadet bargain £20.50. Private room.

Fox and Anchor

Map L4

115 Charterhouse Street, Clerkenwell,
EC1M 6AA **020 7250 1300**
www.foxandanchor.com
⊖ Farringdon
Gastro pub and dining

A beautifully renovated old tavern has
been restored for the 21st century in
Smithfield Market. It serves a great British
menu includes a Maldon raw bar with
Rocks and natives, also steak and oyster
pie. Rock and native – from £9. Wine from
£14.50, Muscadet £17.95. Accommodation.

Galvin La Chapelle

Map N5

35 Spital Square, Spitalfields,
E1 6DY **020 7299 0400**
www.galvinrestaurants.com
⊖ Liverpool Street
French

This large elegant restaurant and '*Bar au
Vin*' prides itself with the finest seasonal
ingredients on menus that change
regularly. Oysters feature quite frequently
in season, so check availability. Oysters –
from £12.50. Wine from £20. Private room.
Al fresco.

Gow's

Map N5

81 – 82 Old Broad Street, City of London,
EC2M 1PR **020 7499 3776**
⊖ Liverpool Street
Fish restaurant and bar

This traditional fish restaurant and oyster
bar has been serving the City for over 100
years. Enjoy the Colchester rock and native
oysters. Rock and native – from £9.25.
Wine from £15.50, Sauvignon Touraine
£19.90. Private room. Closed Saturday and
Sunday.

Green's Restaurant & Oyster Bar

Map M5

14 Cornhill, City of London, EC3V 3ND
020 7220 6300
www.greens.org.uk
⊖ Bank
British

This stylish bar and restaurant is on the
mezzanine overlooking the Royal
Exchange. Sample the West Mersea Rocks
and Natives, and Carlingford Lough Rocks.
Rock and native – from £10.50. Wine from
£19.50, Muscadet £22. Private room.
Closed Saturday and Sunday.

Green's The Runner Bar

Map M5

14 Cornhill, City of London EC3V 3ND
020 7220 6300
www.greens.org.uk
⊖ Bank
Seafood

A large crustacean display is the attraction
at this long curving bar. Sample West
Mersea Rocks and Natives, and
Carlingford Lough Rocks. Rock and native
– from £10.20. Wine from £19.50. Private
room. Closed Saturday and Sunday.

The Gun

Map S6

27 Coldharbour, Docklands, E14 9NS
020 7515 5222
www.thegundocklands.com
⊖ Canary Wharf
Gastro pub

A traditional pub on the banks of the River Thames is now a modern gastro pub and restaurant. An outdoor area overlooking the O2 Arena is ideal for enjoying Brownsea Island Rocks and Duchy Natives. Rock and native – from £12.50. Wine from £16, Muscadet £21. Private room. Al fresco.

Hawksmoor, Spitalfields

Map N4

157 Commercial Street, City of London, E1 6BJ **020 7247 7392**
www.thehawksmoor.co.uk
⊖ Liverpool Street
British steak house

The squeaky porters' trolleys have gone, replaced by a modern British eating scene. Have some saline Cumbrae Rocks, (perhaps with a sizzling sausage), before a tasty steak. The sister restaurant of Hawksmoor Seven Dials. Rock – from £12. Wine from £17, Picpoul de Pinet £19. Private room.

Hix Oyster & Chop House

Map L4

36 – 37 Greenhill Rents, Cowcross Street, Clerkenwell, EC1M 6BN
020 7017 1930
www.hixoysterandchophouse.co.uk
⊖ Farringdon
British

Hix Oyster & Chop House is situated a stones throw from Smithfield Market, London's historic meat market. Originally a sausage factory and then a fish restaurant, many of its original features remain. The wooden floors, marble oyster bar, tiled walls and linen tablecloths go towards creating an elegant yet unfussy dining room. The menu reflects Mark Hix's signature British style with seasonal and daily changing dishes featuring oysters from around the British Isles, sourced by our head chef, and a selection of meats and steaks on the bone.

Hix Oyster & Chop House is in close proximity to the Barbican and Sadler's Wells.

© Jason Lowe

½ dozen oysters and a glass of wine, Monday – Friday between 3 – 7pm, all day Sunday £15.

Oyster and Chop House supports sustainable fishing.

Rock and native – from £13.50. Brownsea Island Rocks, Duchy Natives no.2, Loch Ryan no.1, River Fal no.2. Wine from £20. Al fresco. 🎭 Theatre menu.

Le Bouchon Breton

Map N5

8 Horner Square, Old Spitalfields Market,
Spitalfields, E1 6EW **08000 191704**
www.lebouchonbreton.co.uk
⊖ Liverpool Street
French bistro

On the first floor of Old Spitalfields,
overlooking the market square, this
French traditional bistro specialises in
fruits de mer with oysters from Brittany
and Scotland. Rock – from £11. Wine from
£16. Private hire. Al fresco.

Loch Fyne

Map N5

Leadenhall Market, 77 – 78 Gracechurch
Street, City of London, EC3V 0AS
020 7929 8380
www.lochfyne.com
⊖ Bank
Seafood

In the market at the heart of the City fresh
oysters and other seafood come from pure
Scottish waters delivered daily.
Rock – from £9.50. Wine from £12.95, Gros
Plant £16.95. Closed Saturday and Sunday.

Lutyens

Map L5

85 Fleet Street, EC4Y 1AE
020 7583 8385
www.lutyens-restaurant.com
⊖ St Paul's
Seafood bar and brasserie

This former headquarters of Reuters has
been transformed into a modern bar,
restaurant and club. The light, minimalist
décor of the bar has a shiny nickel bar top
against white walls and marble floor tiles.
Comfortable bar stools and tables are set
for enjoying the delicious bar food that
includes a platter of fruits de mer, a tapas
board, charcuterie and cheese. The
restaurant has an impressive fruits de mer
display and oyster bar where a plate of
natives, rocks, or seafood can be taken.
Traditional brasserie dishes take in aged
beef steaks, seasonal fresh fish including
lobster, bass and turbot, real dishes such
as veal Holstein, calf's liver Lyonnaise, and
poultry and game in season. At the bar
there are Speciales de Claire, Maldons and
Carlingford Lough Natives and Rocks to be
enjoyed, and perhaps cherrystone clams,

scallops and crab. There is an impressive
cellar wine library and lounge bar, with
treasures which start at a modest level
with top selected regional wines at friendly
prices. Service as expected hits the
balance between friendly and formal.

French Speciales, Maldon and West
Mersea Natives. Rock and native – from
£12.50. Wine from £18. Private room.
Closed Saturday and Sunday.

Mercer

Map N5

34 Threadneedle Street,
City of London, EC2R 8AY
020 7628 0001
www.themercer.co.uk
⊖ Bank
British

This modern British restaurant in the heart of the financial district serves a variety of oysters and plenty of seafood. Colchester Natives come in season and Rocks are from Carlingford. Oysters – from £13.75. Wine from £18. Private room. Closed Saturday and Sunday.

The Old Brewery, Greenwich

Map R8

Old Royal Naval College, Greenwich,
SE10 9LW **020 3327 1280**
www.oldbrewerygreenwich.com
⊖ DLR / ⇌ Greenwich
British

Set in the grounds of the Old Royal Naval College at Greenwich next to the Cutty Sark, enjoy Carlingford Lough Rocks, recommended with Meantime London Stout. Rock – from £11. Wine from £15.95. Al fresco.

One New Change Champagne Bar

Map M5

One New Change, First Floor, Cheapside,
EC4M 9AF **020 7871 1213**
www.searcys.co.uk
⊖ St Paul's
Champagne bar

This new Champagne bar is situated on the first floor of the new modernist shopping destination. It has floor to ceiling glass panels with a panoramic lift, and stunning views over St Paul's Cathedral dome. The cuisine takes in new-style tapas and rock oysters to complement the wide selection of Champagne. Rock – from £9. Wine from £23.

Paternoster Chop House

Map M5

Warwick Court, Paternoster Square,
City of London, EC4M 7DX **020 7029 9400**
www.paternosterchophouse.co.uk
⊖ St Paul's
Modern British

Flying the flag for British cuisine the selection of meat and seafood is admirable in this very popular city venue, overlooking St Paul's Cathedral. Sample oysters in the bar from West Mersea, Colchester and Loch Fyne. Rock – from £16.50. Wine from £18.50, Picpoul de Pinet £23.50. Private room. Al fresco. Closed Saturday.

Rivington Greenwich

Map S9

178 Greenwich High Road, Greenwich,
SE10 8NN **020 8293 9270**
www.rivingtongreenwich.co.uk
⇌ Greenwich
British

The sister modern British classic brasserie and gastro bar with Dorset Rocks, West Mersea Natives and angels on horseback. Rock and native – from £12. Wine from £14.50. Private room.

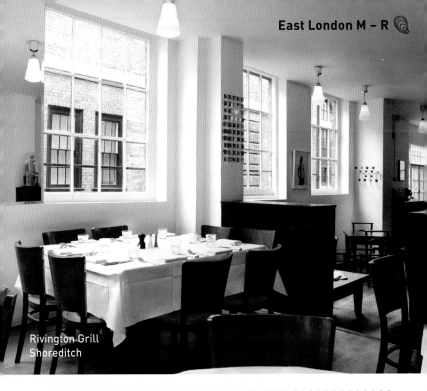

Rivington Grill
Shoreditch

Rivington Grill

Map N4

28 – 30 Rivington Street, Shoreditch,
EC2A 3DZ **020 7729 7053**
www.rivingtongrill.co.uk
Old Street
British gastro bar / brasserie

Everything in this modern gastro bar and
brasserie shines from simple bar snacks
to finest British seafood and meat; sample
herring roes on toast and angels on
horseback, Dorset Rocks and West Mersea
Natives. Rock and native – from £12. Wine
from £17.25. Private room.

Royal Exchange Grand Café

Map M5

The Royal Exchange, Cornhill, EC3V 3LR
020 7618 2480
www.royalexchange-grandcafe.co.uk
Bank
British

Situated in the Grade 1 listed Stock
Exchange building, the original trading
floor is set out with tables, and chic oval
bar. Sample Kumamoto oysters served
with ginger and sesame. Rock and native
– from £11. Wine from £17.50. Private
room. Al fresco. Open Monday – Friday.

St John

Map L4

26 St John Street, Farringdon,
EC1M 4AY **020 7251 0848**
www.stjohnrestaurant.com
⊖ Farringdon
British nose to tail

A former smokehouse near Smithfield Market with simple décor is the backdrop for some of the finest and most interesting British food. Renowned for its nose to tail cuisine, seafood is equally precise with superb langoustines and fine native oysters. Native – from £15. Wine from £21.40 – St John Blanc. Closed Sunday pm.

St John Bread and Wine

Map N5

94 –96 Commercial Street, Spitalfields,
E1 6LZ **020 7251 0848**
www.stjohnbreadandwine.com
⊖ Liverpool Street
British

The sister restaurant has a similar style of food in the now highly popular area of old Spitalfields Market. Seafood, rock oysters and meat dishes excel. Rock – from £11.40. Wine from £21.40, ½ bt Muscadet £14.95.

Searcy's Barbican

Map M5

Level 2 Barbican Centre, Silk Street,
City of London, EC2Y 8DS **020 7588 3008**
www.searcys.co.uk
⊖ Barbican
British

This classic modern British restaurant has delightful views over the Barbican garden and water features. Maldon Rocks make a great pre-theatre snack. Rock – from £12. Wine £23.50. Private room. 🎭 Theatre menu.

Smiths of Smithfield

Map L4

67 –77 Charterhouse Street, Clerkenwell,
EC1M 6HJ **020 7251 7950**
www.smithsofsmithfield.co.uk
⊖ Farringdon
Modern British

On the top floor of this foodie complex, overlooking the converted meat market and with an al fresco terrace for fine weather, Irish Rocks and natives, and Fine de Claires can be enjoyed before the rather meaty main courses. Rock and native – from £16.50. Wine from £13.95. Al fresco.

Sweetings

Map M5

39 Queen Victoria Street, City of London,
EC4N 4SA **020 7248 3062**
⊖ Mansion House
Fish

This City institution since 1889 is perhaps the most traditional seafood restaurant in the area, serving the daily selection of seasonal fish and native oysters in season. Oysters – from £14.25. Wine from £22. Monday – Friday, lunch time only.

Swithins

Map M5

21– 23 Saint Swithin's Lane, City of London, EC4N 8AD **020 7623 6853**
www.swithinsrestaurant.co.uk
⊖ Cannon Street
Wine bar

This elegant champagne bar and seafood restaurant is on the ground floor with an informal basement bar. Sample Rock oyster no.1 with shallot vinegar. Rock – from £7.55. Wine from £12.95, Verginie Sauvignon Blanc £14.50. Private room. Closed on Saturday and Sunday.

The Well

Map L4

180 St John Street, Clerkenwell, EC1V 4JY **020 7251 9363**
www.downthewell.co.uk
⊖ Farringdon
Gastro pub and dining

A refurbished pub in very fashionable Clerkenwell has oysters available as bar snacks or on the restaurant menu. Choose from Cumbrae Rocks and Duchy Natives from Wright Brothers, Borough Market. Rock and native – from £14.50. Wine from £16.50. Private room. Al fresco.

The Well
Clerkenwell

SOUTH LONDON

Balham, Battersea, Bermondsey, Borough, Clapham, Kennington, Putney, South Bank, Southwark, Stockwell, Wandsworth, Waterloo

. . . .

Applebee's Borough Market   Map M6

5 Stoney Street, Borough, SE1 9AA
020 7407 5777
www.applebeesfish.com
⊖ London Bridge
Fishmonger and café restaurant

On the edge of bustling Borough Market this pristine fishmongers has a glistening counter and an in-shop café to enjoy freshly cooked seafood dishes or plate of rock oysters. Oysters – from £12. Wine from £17. Private hire. Al fresco. Closed Sunday, Monday.

. . . .

The Avalon   Map i11

16 Balham Hill, Wandsworth,
SW12 9EB **020 8675 8613**
www.theavalonlondon.com
⊖ Clapham South
Gastro pub

This modern bar with dining room has a daily chalkboard menu with specialities including fresh rock oysters from Wright Brothers. Rock – from £12.50. Wine from £14. Private room. Al fresco.

. . . .

Bar Estrela   Map K9

113 –115 South Lambeth Road, Stockwell,
SW8 1UZ **020 7793 1051**
⊖ Stockwell
Portuguese bistro

In 'little Portugal' in South Lambeth this bustling bar and restaurant has a seafood counter. Indulge in the very fair prices, whilst watching soccer and sport on big screens. There's a big outside area and a separate restaurant for the quieter diners. Rock oysters £4.80 – bargain of the guide! Wine from £11. Al fresco.

. . . .

Bennett Oyster Bar & Brasserie   Map G9

7 – 9 Battersea Square, Battersea,
W11 3RA **020 7223 5545**
www.bennettsbrasserie.com
⊖ Imperial Wharf
British seafood brassiere & oyster bar

This impressive new seafood brasserie has an oyster bar where natives and rocks come from Ireland, Dorset and Jersey from Rossmore Oysters. Rock and native – from £8.40. Wine from £17.

Butlers Wharf Chop House

Map N6

Butlers Wharf Building,
36e Shad Thames, SE1 2YE
020 7403 3403
www.chophouse-restaurant.co.uk
⊖ London Bridge / Tower Hill
Modern British

Overlooking Tower Bridge with the Thames gliding at its own sweet will, a plate of Maldon oysters at the bar or table makes a great start to the carnivorous modern British menu. Rock – from £9.75. Wine from £20, Muscadet £28.

Fish and Grill, Putney

Map E10

200 – 204 Putney Bridge Road, Putney,
SW15 2NA **020 8246 4140**
www.fishandgrillputney.co.uk
⊖ Putney Bridge
Seafood

The modern interior and a display of fresh fish sets the scene for a great seafood experience, including Poole Bay rock oysters; the love of finest produce and enthusiasm drives this now expanding group. Rock – from £11.95. Wine from £16, Stellenbosch £19.50. Private room.

The Fish Club, Clapham

Map J10

57 Clapham High Street, Clapham,
SW4 7TG **020 7720 5853**
www.thefishclub.com
⊖ Clapham Common
Fish and Chip Shop

This innovative take on the traditional fish and chip shop has a daily fish display with contemporary café-style dining. Rock and native – from £9.95. Wine from £13.95.

The Fish Club, Clapham Junction

Map G10

189 St John's Hill, Clapham Junction,
SW11 1TH **020 7978 7115**
www.thefishclub.com
⇌ Clapham Junction
Fish and Chips

The strap line of 'the future of fish and chips' is appropriate as you can start with perhaps smoked sprats, Rock or native oysters, crayfish cocktail and then select from a wide range of grilled or deep-fried fish including coley, haddock, cuttlefish and bream. Rock and native – from £9.95. Wine from £13.95.

Fish Kitchen, Borough Market

Map M6

Cathedral Street, Borough Market,
Borough, SE1 9AL **020 7407 3803**
www.fishkitchen.com
⊖ London Bridge
Fish

On the corner of bustling Borough Market this modern seafood restaurant is set in a conservatory with a large al fresco area and takeaway shop. Fine fresh fish simply delivered include fresh Bigbury Bay rock oysters. Rock – from £11.70. Wine from £16.95. Al fresco.

Gastro

Map J10

67 Venn Street, Clapham, SW4 0BD
020 7627 0222
⊖ Clapham Common
French brasserie

This bar brasserie transports diners to a truly Gaelic experience with unashamedly French food, oysters and wine in a relaxed ambience. Rock – from £9.90. Wine from £16. Private room. Al fresco.

Harrison's

Map i12

15 –19 Bedford Hill, Balham,
SW12 9EX **020 8675 6900**
www.harrisonsbalham.co.uk
⊖ Balham
European bar and restaurant

This impressive modern British bar and restaurant has stunning décor and is a great setting for Maldon rock oysters, fresh fish and estate meat in a relaxed ambience with spot-on service.
Rock – from £12. Wine from £14.50. Private room. Al fresco.

La Rueda, Clapham

Map J10

66 - 68 Clapham High Street, Clapham,
SW4 7UL **020 7627 2173**
www.larueda-restaurant.com
⊖ Clapham North
Spanish

This long-standing Spanish tapas bar is reminiscent of many bars in the Ramblas or La Loja. Oysters feature among the long list of traditional tapas to be eaten at the bar or served at tables. Rock – from £7.50. Wine from £12.95, Torres Vina Sol £15.50. Private hire. Al fresco.

La Terraza

Map K10

27 – 31 Bedford Road, Clapham North,
SW4 7SH **020 7737 4066**
www.laterraza.co.uk
⊖ Clapham North
Spanish

This authentic Spanish tapas bar and restaurant has a long list of traditional tapas with rock oysters served singly to complete a selection. Rock – from £7.80. Wine from £14.50, Torres Vina Sol £14.50. Al fresco.

Le Bouchon Bordelais

Map H10

5 – 9 Battersea Rise, Clapham,
SW11 1HG **020 7738 0307**
www.lebouchon.co.uk
⇌ Clapham Junction
French bistro

Burgundy awnings set off this bustling French brasserie with its mirror walls and large terrace. Dorset Rocks are part of the very French provincial menu. Rock – from £10.80. Wine from £15 - Sauvignon Blanc. Private hire. Al fresco.

Le Pont de la Tour Bar & Grill

Map N6

The Butlers Wharf Building,
36d Shad Thames, Tooley Street,
SE1 2YE **020 7403 8403**
www.lepontdelatour.com
⊖ London Bridge / Tower Hill
Modern British

This glamorous riverside setting, facing
Tower Bridge, has a seafood counter, bar
and restaurant, as one would expect in a
top Parisian brasserie. Classic modern
cuisine takes in seafood, meat and game
with Maldon rock and native oysters.
Rock and native – from £11.50. Wine from
£26. Private room. Al fresco.

Livebait, Waterloo

Map L6

43 The Cut, Waterloo, SE1 8LF
0844 692 3901
www.livebaitrestaurants.co.uk
⊖ Southwark
Fish

Livebait, Waterloo offers a great range of
fresh fish and seafood, cooked to
perfection every time. Located in The Cut
and within a 2 minutes walk from the Old
and Young Vic theatres, the Waterloo
restaurant is ideal for pre-theatre dining.

Only ethically-sourced fish is served and
the restaurant supports sustainable
fishing policies, providing the freshest
seafood with a minimal impact on the
environment. The ever-changing catch of
the day ranges from gilthead bream to
bass, Cornish sardines, generous plates of
tuna and classic fish and chips which is
simply a must to try. Their international
wine won't disappoint with a massive

selection of wines to choose from, or why
not try a refreshing Bloody Mary which
perfectly complements the fresh oysters.

Rock – from £9.50. Wine from £17,
Muscadet £22. 🎭 Theatre menu.

Lobster Pot

Map L7

3 Kennington Lane, Kennington,
SE11 4RG **020 7582 5556**
www.lobsterpotrestaurant.co.uk
⊖ Kennington
Brittany-style French fish

Complete with eccentric French proprietor,
fish tanks and the sound of the sea and
seagulls, this long-time favourite offers a
host of produce from the sea including
Colchester Rocks and Natives. Try oysters
au gratin with champagne sauce. Rock
and native – from £9.50. Wine from £17.50.

Oxo Tower

Map L6

Oxo Tower Wharf, Barge House Street,
South Bank, SE1 9PH
020 7803 3888
www.harveynichols.com
⊖ Waterloo
Modern British / pan – Asian

With stunning views over the river and the
City, with a 250ft terrace, restaurant,
brasserie and bar, this is a place to savour
the modern pan Asian and British cuisine.
Enjoy oysters at the bar or perhaps
Japanese-style deep-fried oysters.
Rock – from £10.50. Wine from £20.

Roast

Map M6

The Floral Hall, Borough Market, Stoney
Street, Southwark, SE1 1TL
0845 034 7300
www.roast-restaurant.com
⊖ London Bridge
British

In a beautiful room sitting over Borough
Market the food is resolutely British as one
would expect, serving skilful cuisine and
the freshest Loch Fyne oysters. Rock –
from £13.50. Wine from £25 - Chilean
Chardonnay.

Tsunami

Map J10

5 –7 Voltaire Road, Clapham,
SW4 6DQ **020 7978 1610**
www.tsunamirestaurant.co.uk
⊖ Clapham North
Japanese

This modern Japanese restaurant serves
oysters in hot olive oil with ponzu in its
'sunkiss seafood' selection, and oyster
shooter with sake, ponzu, momiji oroshi,
quail egg and scallion. Wow!
Rock – from £12.50. Wine from £16.50.

Village East

Map N7

171 –173 Bermondsey Street,
Bermondsey, SE1 3UW
020 7357 6082
www.villageeast.co.uk
⊖ London Bridge
Modern European

In bustling Bermondsey, set in a modern
warehouse development with an open
kitchen, oysters are available at the bar
and in the restaurant. Try with shallot
vinegar or with soy mirrin dressing.
Rock – from £8.50. Wine from £15.
Private room.

Wright Brothers Oyster & Porter House

Map M6

11 Stoney Street, Borough Market,
Southwark, SE1 9AD **020 7403 9554**
www.wrightbrothersoysterhouse.com
⊖ London Bridge
Seafood

Walking into Wright Brothers oyster bar in Borough Market is akin to revisiting the Victorian era. The dark green wood and solid bar with oyster wheels for placing a platter is typical of many raw bars that were the haunts of gentlemen with mutton chops and bowler hats. However the clientele is remarkably varied with many younger groups showing oysters are popular with this generation. Behind the bar are the oyster shuckers and chefs beavering away and there's plenty of fire as they sizzle platters under the grill. Ale and porter fit the scene of Borough Market as this was the tipple of the market porters. Muscadet and Picpoul de Pinet are favourites of the wine imbibers, and there's plenty to choose at user-friendly prices. There is nowhere to match the mouth-watering list of the several different oysters to choose from, served glistening on the half shell, such as Duchy, Cumbrae, Carlingford, Brownsea Island and West Mersea and the adventurous list of oyster dishes, with the classics Kilpatrick and

Rockefeller along side oysters Japanese or oysters and spicy chorizo. The specials board changes daily with the day boat fish that have arrived in the morning and there are the Wright Brothers house staples, beef Guinness and oyster pie, magnificent fruit de mers and pints of Atlantic prawns. There is always a friendly bustle as staff serve with speed and the smiling faces of the chefs keeps regulars coming back again and again.

Rock and native – from £11.50. Rock oysters, Speciale de Claire, native, Oyster Kilpatrick, New Orleans, Spanish, Japanese. Wine from £23.

WEST LONDON

Chiswick, East Sheen, Richmond, Sheen, Shepherd's Bush

· ·

Anglesea Arms

Map C6

35 Wingate Road, Shepherd's Bush,
W6 0UR **020 8749 1291**
⊖ Ravenscourt Park
Gastro pub

A long-established free house gastro pub with unpretentious delicious home-cooked seasonal food in a great ambience. Rock – from £9.95. Wine from £15.50. Al fresco.

· ·

Fish Kitchen, East Sheen

Map C10

170 Upper Richmond Road, East Sheen,
SW14 8AW **020 8878 1040**
www.fishkitchen.com
⇌ Mortlake
Fish

Sleek black tiles, slate, wood flooring and smart banquette seating sets the theme for a classy fish experience. Fresh fish, simply cooked is popular. Try halibut, bass, scallops, tuna or rock oysters.
Rocks – from £9.95. Wine from £14.95.

· ·

Fishworks, Richmond

13 – 19 The Square, Richmond, Surrey,
TW9 1EA **020 8948 5965**
www.fishworks.co.uk
⇌ Richmond
Fish

The company theme of a seafood restaurant and fishmonger serves natives and rock oysters from Maldon and Colchester. Rock – from £9. Wine from £16.50, Muscadet £20.

· ·

Le Vacherin

Map B7

76 South Parade, Chiswick,
W4 5LF **020 8742 2121**
www.levacherin.com
⊖ Chiswick Park
French

This traditional French brasserie, specialising in baked vacherin and some very traditional dishes, has Strangford Lough Rocks as part of the French repertoire. Rock – part of prix fix 3 course menu. Wine from £17.95, Sauvignon Côtes du Tarn £19.95. Private room.

Sam's Brasserie

Map B7

11 Barley Mow Passage, Chiswick,
W4 4PH **020 8987 0555**
www.samsbrasserie.co.uk
⊖ Chiswick Park
Modern European

Sister restaurant to Harrison's in Balham,
this modern European restaurant serves
Colchester rock oysters on its eclectic
menu. Rock – from £12. Wine from £15.

Victoria

Map A10

10 West Temple, Sheen, SW14 7RT
020 8876 4238
www.thevictoria.net
⇌ Sheen
Modern British

This refurbished gastro pub now with
dining and rooms has a thoroughly British
menu that includes Jersey Rocks on a
good value menu. Rock – from £9.90. Wine
from £16. Al fresco. Accommodation.

Le Vacherin
Chiswick

GREATER LONDON

Croydon, Gatwick, Hounslow, Kingston upon Thames, Sutton

Caviar House & Prunier at London Airports

Gatwick Airport Terminal North & South
Gatwick Airport, Gatwick,
West Sussex, RH6 0PJ

Heathrow Airport Terminal 1, 2, 3, 4 & 5
Heathrow Airport, Hounslow,
Middlesex, TW6 2BA

www.caviarhouse-prunier.com

Relax preflight at these stylish seafood bars. A plate of rock oysters will set you up for a long haul, or keep the palate fresh for arrival at European destinations. Sample the wonderful Balik smoked salmon, Alaska King crab, dressed Cornish crab, lobster, langoustines, crevettes and the generous rock oysters. These are served singly or various platters and wash down with a glass of Champagne, Chablis or Muscadet.

Brasserie Vacherin

12 High Street, Sutton, Surrey, SM1 1HN
020 8722 0180
www.brasserievacherin.co.uk
⇌ Sutton
French brasserie

The more casual cousin of the Chiswick fine dining restaurant serves brasserie-style food with the vacherin as the star alongside Strangford Lough rock oysters. Rock – from £9.95. Wine from £16.

Fish Kitchen, Kingston

58 Coombe Road, Kingston upon Thames, Surrey, KT2 7AF **020 8546 2886**
www.fishkitchen.com
⇌ Norbiton
Fish

A new extension to the renowned fishmonger Jarvis of Kingston, the freshest fish is what marks this fish and chip experience from the rest. A smart decked area is for al fresco eating. Try rock oysters then fish grilled or deep-fried with chips and mushy peas. Rock – from £9.95. Wine £14.95. Al fresco.

Fish and Grill, Croydon

48 – 50 South End, Croydon, CR0 1DP
020 8774 4060
www.fishandgrill.co.uk
⇌ South Croydon
Seafood

The modern interior and a display of the fresh fish sets the scene for a great seafood experience including Poole Bay rock oysters; the love of finest produce and enthusiasm drives this now expanding group. Rock – from £11.95. Wine from £16, Stellenbosch £19.50. Private room.

There are over 30 UK
species of oyster to try.

Colchester Oyster Fishery

Colchester Oyster Fishery is one of the United Kingdom's leading suppliers of fresh shellfish and has built its name and reputation in the industry over more than 40 years as being a quality live shellfish supplier. This has resulted in our customer base including wholesalers such as Billingsgate Fish Market, and many of the finest London restaurants and hotels. We also supply the public via our website or direct from the Fishery door Monday – Friday 09.00 – 16.30.

Established in 1964, to grow and supply the Colchester Native Oyster and Rock Oysters, our oyster beds have a history that dates back to 1189. In an age when much of the food we eat is the subject of controversial methods of rearing and preserving, we are proud to be a company that delivers fresh products without the need for any additives or preservatives.

The Fishery is based on Mersea Island, a small island 8 miles south of Colchester, connected to the mainland by a causeway that is covered at springtides. At this location overlooking the Pyefleet Creek, surrounded by unspoilt salt marshes and a bird sanctuary we grow, grade and store our shellfish.

Colchester Oyster Fishery
01206 384141
www.colchesteroysterfishery.com

Loch Fyne Oysters

Loch Fyne Oysters are grown in Ardkinglas at the head of Loch Fyne, West Scotland, and by our partner growers in Argyll and the Islands. Different sites have their peak seasons at different times of the year: the Ardkinglas oysters from spring until early winter, and the Islands in winter.

The Island oysters come from Andy Abrahams, who grows his shellfish on the strand on Colonsay, where the wind whips in across the Atlantic, all the way from New York. Oysters also come from Tony Archibald, from his site on the shore at Loch Grunart on Islay. These fisheries are excellent partners for Loch Fyne.

The Loch Fyne business began as a small lochside oyster bar– a venture by Johnny Noble, the owner of the Ardkinglas Estate, and his colleague Andy Lane. Both were oyster enthusiasts, and they began selling them to UK restaurants. They opened their own oyster bar in

1988 and UK tourists commented on how popular the concept would be 'back home'. In 1990 the Loch Fyne Oyster Bar opened in Nottingham. In 1998 Loch Fyne Restaurants was founded. There are now 41 restaurants across the UK, as well as the original Oyster Bar in Cairndow which is now a major tourist attraction.

Loch Fyne Oysters
Clachan, Cairndow,
Argyll PA26 8BL
www.lochfyne.com

Taittinger Champagne

Renowned for the quality and elegance of their Champagnes, the Taittinger family has been rooted in Champagne since 1931. Headed up by Pierre Emmanuel Taittinger, Taittinger Champagne remains one of the few Grandes Marques to be actively managed by the family named on the label.

The hallmark of their wines is the high percentage of Chardonnay they contain; this gives the wines delicacy and finesse. Their top prestige cuvée, the Comtes de Champagne Blanc de Blancs has been coined as the ultimate Chardonnay. This remarkable Champagne was James Bond's Champagne of choice in the book Casino Royale.

This Champagne along with the family's signature cuvée, Taittinger Brut Réserve are widely available in London bars and restaurants. Both Champagnes would be perfect matches for fresh oysters with a dash of Tabasco and sublime with tempura style oysters.

Bodegas Hidalgo

Bodegas Hidalgo is in its sixth generation and is widely regarded as the definitive Manzanilla house. Extensive vineyard holdings ensure the best quality Palomino Fino is delivered from the bright albariza soils to the bodegas in Sanlúcar de Barrameda, where every step is taken during the long solera process to deliver excellence and consistency.

'Manzanilla, produced in the town of Sanlúcar de Barrameda, is generally speaking the lightest style of sherry, with a saline tang thought to derive from the position of the barrel cellars near to the sea. La Gitana is a great introduction to its refreshing charms; dry. Crisp, clean, and with a hint of that savoury saline character, it's best served chilled.'

Observer.guardian.co.uk,
13 March 2011

Widely available at £9 in Majestic Wine Warehouses, Tesco and Waitrose.

Rossmore Oysters Ltd.

Rossmore Oysters has been supplying London's top chefs since 1969. Based in Sussex, they are able to deliver the freshest selection of rock and native Oysters from around our coast, daily to London.

The company has formed a partnership with the Wallace family in Loch Ryan, to revive their oyster beds and provide the only Scottish Native Oyster in the market. The eight stainless steel depuration tanks can hold 50,000 oysters, and the oysters are packed with total traceability.

They have achieved the SALSA certificate for food safety, a complete food safety system, ensuring a safe product every time.

The regular contact the company has with its farmers, ensures the changing selection of oysters that are supplied are of the highest quality and always in good condition. They are handled to exacting health standards, packed beautifully, and delivered on time.

Rossmore Oysters Ltd.
Lakeview, Old Hollow, Worth,
Sussex RH10 4TA
01293 888868
tristan@oysters.co.uk
www.oysters.co.uk

The Loch Ryan Oyster Fishery Co Ltd.

Loch Ryan is a shallow, 13km long Loch in South West Scotland near Stranraer, producing plump oysters, with a light nutty taste, and strong shell.

It is Scotland's largest native oyster bed, producing about 400,000 oysters every year. Growth in the Loch is slow, at about 10g / year, so the harvested oysters are about 10 years old. Only the largest 5% of the catch is sold, and the smallest are re-laid into well marked, dense beds for future years. The Scottish Government and Scottish Water have keenly supported the oyster bed, to ensure the water quality is of the highest standard, and is protected for future years.

Walter Speirs, Chairman, Association of Scottish Shellfish Growers, says: "These beds should have a productive and prosperous future, and are a good example of how native oyster beds can be managed. They remain one of the most important native oyster beds in Scotland today." Andrew Fairlie, executive head chef of Gleneagles, says, "We have been serving Loch Ryan Native Oysters to our guests at the restaurant for years now and we are very lucky to have access to a true delicacy. It's a product that Scotland should be very proud of."

The Loch Ryan Oyster Fishery Co Ltd.
C/o The Thatched Cottage, Penberth, St. Buryan, Penzance, Cornwall TR19 6HJ
07887 575747
sales@lochryanoysters.com
www.lochryanoysters.com

Maldon

The Maldon Oyster Company is based close to the Maldon Salt Company and benefits from the same wonderful stretch of waterway the Blackwater Estuary. The six miles from Maldon town to the Virley Channel and West Mersea is known to be some of the finest terroir for oyster cultivation in Britain. Oysters have been fished here since Roman times. They founded the town of Colchester and the area has since been renowned for the finest plump native oysters.

Since the introduction and cultivation of the Pacific or rock oyster into Britain the main development has been with this species. The waters are rich in natural plankton that feeds the oysters so they grow to market size in two seasons, as compared to at least four for natives.

The hatchery reared spat or baby oysters are put on strategically sited oyster trestles in mesh bags so they can grow without being washed away. Larger oysters are then sited in the best lays within the Blackwater Estuary where they can grow to market size.

Wild native oysters are dredged from the waters off Colne Point and Dengie Flats and these are re-laid into the beds in the Blackwater. Both the rock and native oysters are purified in specialist tanks before they are marketed in London.

Maldon Oyster Company attends the farmers' market in Duke of York Square Kings Road every Saturday or by direct contact for trade customers.

Maldon Oyster Company
Birchwood Farm, Cock Clarks, Chelmsford CM3 6RF
01621 828 699
sales@maldonoyster.com
www.maldonoyster.com

Duchy Oyster Farm

The Duchy of Cornwall Oyster Farm, situated on the Helford River in South West Cornwall, is an ancient private fishery, part of the private estate of the Duke of Cornwall, HRH The Prince of Wales. Helford River native oysters have been renowned for generations and were delivered far and wide throughout Britain to numerous restaurants.

Wright brothers took over the fishery in 2005 and began an ambitious regeneration project assisted by a European fisheries subsidy. They now cultivate and harvest over ten million native and pacific oysters per annum, making the Duchy Oyster Farm one of the largest oyster farms in the UK.

Wright's Bros Wholesalers based in London's Borough Market is the largest supplier of oysters to London restaurants, the first independent merchant to establish for over thirty years.

The oysters stocked on a daily basis include Colchester natives, wild Colchester rocks, Maldon native and rocks, Japanese Kumomoto, Brownsea Island rocks and natives, with rock oysters from Portland, Carlingford, Lindisfarne, Cumbrae and Isle of Ilay. Other molluscs include live cherrystone clams, palourdes and razor clams. Prepared crustaceans such as crab meat, peeled brown shrimps and crayfish tails and whole crevettes and Hedderman smoked salmon complete their service.

They supply their own outlets Wright Brothers in Soho and in Borough Market, plus numerous other oyster bars and restaurants throughout London.

Duchy Oyster Farm
Port Navas, Falmouth,
Cornwall TR11 5RJ
01326 340210
info@duchyoysterfarm.com
www.duchyoysterfarm.com

The Jersey Oyster Company

Looking down from Mont Orgueil Castle into the waters of the Royal Bay of Grouville it's easy to see why Jersey oysters are so fresh. With some of the best water quality in Europe our oysters are able to thrive in an organic environment and when the sea is this clean, that's something very special.

The Jersey Oyster Company is owned and run by Mr Chris Le Masurier, a third generation Jersey oyster farmer. The Company's shore based activity is conducted within a short distance of beach production areas, at the property where Mr Le Masurier's grandfather commenced an aquaculture business over forty years ago. Since 1999 the Company has undergone an intensive expansion programme and now maintains over 35 hectares of 'beach concession' areas, located off Jersey's south-east coast.

Oysters are held on small sites close to the shore before export, where they spend at least half the day exposed when the tide is out to "harden" them. This ensures minimal stress levels during transport and maximum shelf-life to maintain a supremely fresh flavour.

The construction of new 'state of the art' premises in 2011 has enabled the business to build on its reputation as a supplier and exporter of the highest quality oysters. The new facility allows produce to meet stringent standards of hygiene and product traceability which are demanded by discerning customers.

The Jersey Oyster Company
La Ferme, La Grande Route des Sabons, Grouville, Jersey JE3 9FE
01534 852553
info@jerseyoyster.com
www.jerseyoyster.com

Richard Haward's Oysters

The Haward family have been growing oysters in the creeks around Mersea Island since the eighteenth century when Wm. Haward sailed with oysters to Billingsgate. From the start of September, they would dredge the natives from the laying; only taking those which were large enough for sale, whilst returning the small to grow for another year or more. They would also look after the oysters, parting them from the larger oyster or cultch, i.e. piece of shell, they had settled on and taking out the "fivefingers", i.e. starfish, and oyster drill, both of which would happily kill and eat oysters.

Today, life is similar, but they are more involved with rock oysters, which now breed prolifically and survive much better than the native, whose numbers are greatly diminished. They now retail many of their oysters at places such as

Borough Market and the "Company Shed" and wholesaling them through the UK and the rest of the world. The Company Shed, which opened in the late 1980's to just sell shellfish to take away at weekends has grown, Topsylike, to become world-renowned as the place to eat Colchester Natives as well as a wide range of other fish and shellfish.

Richard Haward's Oysters
129 Coast Road, West Mersea, Colchester, Essex CO5 8PA
01206 383284
enquiries@richardhawardsoysters.co.uk
www.richardhawardsoysters.co.uk

Dorset Oysters

Dorset Oysters Limited was set up by Pete Miles fisherman, cook and restaurateur in 2009 when he couldn't buy local oysters for his restaurant Storm in Poole. Poole has some of the biggest beds in the country and the oysters are of prime quality but most of these were sent abroad to the French and Asian markets. Originally the idea was just to supply the Storm restaurant but soon he discovered there was a huge demand for Poole oysters. He then built a state of the art depuration plant to purify and market rock and native oysters, palourde clam and cockle.

Rock oysters grow on the shores of Brownsea Island and have a good meat content with a lively mineral flavour.

Palourde clams and Poole cockles are harvested by specialist fisherman committed to a responsible fishing scheme.

The clams are of premium quality, and the cockles are considered the best in the world.

Dorset Oysters Limited
13 Benson Road,
Nuffield Trading Estate,
Poole, Dorset BH13 0GB
01202 666057
www.dorsetoysters.com
www.stormfishrestaurant.co.uk

OYSTERS
READY TO EAT NOW

£3·50 ½ DOZ

£6·50 1 DOZ

NUTRITION

Oysters and health

Health benefits of oysters

- Oysters provide proteins, vitamins and minerals
- They are low in saturated fat and calories
- A great source of Omega 3
- Varied types which have different health benefits
- Rich in Zinc, Vitamin B12 and Copper
- Good source of Iron, Vitamin D and Iodine

Omega-3

Omega-3 is a type of fat found in oil-rich seafood. They can help to protect the heart, and are believed to reduce the risks of developing some forms of cancer. However, Omega-3 cannot be made in the body, so a dietary supply is essential.

Eating foods which are naturally rich remains the best way to up your intake, and most species of shellfish are either 'rich' or 'good' sources. Six rock oysters represent 43% of your recommended weekly intake of Omega-3. Six native oysters represent 40% of your recommended weekly intake of Omega-3.

Oysters and Vitamins

Zinc helps to process the carbohydrate, fat and protein in the food we eat, and assists with the healing of wounds.

Copper helps to produce red and white blood cells, and triggers the release of iron to form haemoglobin. It is important for infant growth, brain development, the immune system and for strong bones.

Vitamin B12 is important for healthy brain and nervous system function, and plays a key role in red blood cell formation.

Iron is key to making the red blood cells that carry oxygen around the body. Iron deficiency can result in anaemia.

Vitamin D helps to regulate the amount of calcium and phosphate in the body, keeping bone and teeth healthy.

Iodine, naturally present in seawater, is a key constituent of thyroid hormones. These are essential for the good functioning of the metabolic rate and healthy cells.

Oysters and Cholesterol

Cholesterol is a fat made by the body. A certain amount is healthy, but too much increases the risk of cardiovascular disease.

Oyster nutrition

 Fat
1.3g | 1.9% RDA

 Sugars
Trace | 0% RDA

65 **Calories**
3.3% RDA

Low **Saturated Fat**
0.2g | 1.0% RDA

 Salt
1.28g | 21.3% RDA

(Per 100g serving)

Cholesterol comes in two types:

1. Blood cholesterol – the amount of cholesterol in the bloodstream

2. Dietary cholesterol – the amount of cholesterol present in the foods we eat.

Dietary cholesterol is not the main cause of high blood cholesterol. Genetic factors also play a part, affecting the absorption, manufacture and uptake of cholesterol.

Foods that have high saturated fat levels have a greater effect in raising blood cholesterol than dietary cholesterol. Foods high in saturated fat include processed meats, full-fat dairy foods, cakes, biscuits, pastry, and puddings. Replacing these with lower fat dairy foods, lean meat and seafood will lower your amount of saturated fat.

Previously, those with high cholesterol were told to avoid oysters due to the dietary cholesterol that is present. The levels of dietary cholesterol in oysters is about half as much as in chicken, and they contain very little fat. For most people they do not cause a rise in cholesterol levels, and do not need to be avoided.

Moderate consumption of oysters as part of a balanced diet should not pose a problem. However, for those with Familial Hypercholesterolaemia (FH) or Familial Combined Hyperlipidaemia (FCH), dietary cholesterol may need to be more carefully managed. These are forms of inherited high cholesterol which occur in 1 in 100 people. People with FH or FCH often have unusually high levels of blood cholesterol, and are more sensitive to changes in dietary cholesterol.

Glorious oysters

• •

Oyster types

Native and rock oysters are distinctively different, but they also vary significantly according to their precise origin.

Most oyster fisheries are located where native oysters have been fished for centuries. The river estuaries of East Anglia and Kent have been traditional fisheries since Roman days. The ria coastline of Cornwall and Devon, the Helford, Fal, Fowey and Dart rivers have had thriving natural stocks. In Scotland many of the waterways, particularly Loch Ryan and Loch Fyne and many of the islands, have abundant native oysters on their shores. Many of these areas have also cultivated the rock oyster which grows successfully on their beds. For many the rock oyster, with its fast growth is the main variety on offer.

Each oyster bed produces a character that is marked by its shell growth and rock oysters in particular have notable differences from fishery to fishery. The native oyster has a regular and concentric shell growth and hence more even in shape. But a keen oyster eye will soon spot the difference between a Colchester and a Helford, a Loch Ryan from a Whitstable and from the other beds around the coastline. Some natives have a definite blue tinge to the flat shell, particularly from West Mersea or Loch Ryan. A Helford often has notable crusted growth from

various marine organisms, and the shell can be tinged inside with bronze and mahogany perhaps from the mineral content of the water. A native from the River Colne in Colchester usually has a pure white inside shell.

The rock oyster will vary in shape considerably, often with very flared shells, some are more elongated, some deeper. A Jersey Rock benefits from the pure waters from the Atlantic, and the huge tidal range that leaves them exposed daily at low tide. The shell growth is hence solid and robust, with sweet fish inside.

Oysters feed by filtering water through their system – a single oyster can filter up to 10 litres of water per hour. The flavour of oysters is a function of the minerals, salinity, and the type of algae they eat in the water. A fully saline oyster will have a very briny taste while oysters with very low salinity can taste flat, almost buttery.

The flavour of each oyster is distinctive to its terroir, but it is the personal preference of every oyster lover which they favour. For me any oyster that is fresh and in good seasonal condition is delicious. The whole joy over the years has been to sample as many different ones as possible. The following few pages show some of the variations you might encounter within a small selection of beds from around the UK.

Glorious oysters

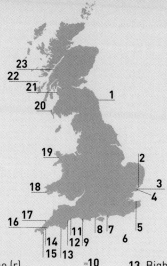

1. Lindisfarne (r)
2. West Mersea (r / n)
3. River Exe (r)
4. Maldon (r / n)
5. Whitstable (r)
6. English Channel (n)
7. Portsmouth Harbour (n)
8. Poole (r)
9. Fleet (n)
10. Jersey (r)
11. Colchester (r)
12. River Teign (r)

13. Bigbury Bay (r)
14. Frenchman's Creek (r)
15. Duchy Special (r)
16. Fal (r / n)
17. Camel (r)
18. Milford Haven (n)
19. Menai (r)
20. Loch Ryan (n)
21. Cumbrae (r)
22. Colonsay (r)
23. Caledonian (r)

Rock oyster (r) Native oyster (n)

Oyster taste guide (to be used with pages 84 – 96)

Flavour ①—②—③—④—⑤—⑥—⑦—⑧—⑨
Light   Full flavoured

Saltiness ①—②—③—④—⑤—⑥—⑦—⑧—⑨
Neutral   Briny

Sweetness ①—②—③—④—⑤—⑥—⑦—⑧—⑨
Neutral   Strong sweetness

Umami* ①—②—③—④—⑤—⑥—⑦—⑧—⑨
Mild   Strong

*Umami (the Japanese word meaning "the essence of deliciousness") is a fifth category of taste, separate from the familiar quartet of sweet, salty, sour, and bitter. Umami is perhaps best described as savoury. It's what makes chicken broth & soy sauce 'meaty'. Free amino acids, especially glutamate, are responsible for umami. When an oyster is called brothy, that's umami. A thin oyster can still have plenty of umami.

Rock oysters

Bigbury Bay

5 Flavour **4** Saltiness **3** Sweetness **3** Umami

Nose A neutral nose but edging towards brackish.

Body Quite distinct parsley and cut grass.

Finish A short clean earthy copper finish.

Texture Full and plump.

Caledonian (Loch Creran)

8 Flavour **4** Saltiness **8** Sweetness **5** Umami

Nose Floral; akin to samphire.

Body Big fruity flavours of apples, pears and avocado.

Finish Initially sweet but culminates with tangy tin.

Texture Plump and silky.

Camel

7 Flavour **4** Saltiness **7** Sweetness **8** Umami

Nose Seaweed and rockpools.

Body Cucumber and lettuce with a touch of lemon juice.

Finish Sharp metallic zing in the midst of soothing sweetness.

Texture Smooth and silky.

Colchester

8 Flavour **7** Saltiness **3** Sweetness **7** Umami

Nose The smell of the open sea; iodine and ozone.

Body A very clear flavour of salted butter.

Finish A metallic finish with potting soil and mushroom essence.

Texture Firm and creamy.

ROCK
Colchester

One of the most famous
areas in Europe for native
and rock oysters. These
rocks are full of flavour
with iodine, butter, mineral
and mushroom notes.

OYSTER TYPES

Rock oysters

Colonsay

7 Flavour **4** Saltiness **7** Sweetness **5** Umami

Nose Very slight sea breeze and geranium.
Body Woody and nutty; avocado and pecan.

Finish Strong white sugar finish.
Texture Meaty.

Cumbrae

7 Flavour **6** Saltiness **6** Sweetness **8** Umami

Nose An established salty nose.
Body A deep flavour of wood and nuts.

Finish Slow coming but a durable copper hit.
Texture Firm and meaty.

Duchy Special (Helford)

8 Flavour **5** Saltiness **7** Sweetness **7** Umami

Nose A light neutral nose.
Body Succulent cashew nutty taste with a noticeable sweetness.

Finish An intense quick finish of brown sugar and copper.
Texture Firm, meaty and plump.

Fal

7 Flavour **3** Saltiness **4** Sweetness **7** Umami

Nose Very delicate saltwater.
Body A manifest nutty taste.

Finish A neat and tidy burst of sweetness that quickly recedes.
Texture Plump, meaty and creamy.

ROCK
Poole

The flow of water through
the natural waterway of
Poole Harbour induces fast
regular growth and full
plump oysters with a nutty,
buttery, slightly earthy
taste over saline and
cucumber freshness.
(See page 90)

OYSTER TYPES

Rock oysters

• •

Frenchman's Creek (Helford)

7 Flavour **5** Saltiness **6** Sweetness **5** Umami

Nose A delicate nose suggestive of samphire and geranium.

Body Deep sweet nutty flavour. Hint of cashews and brown sugar.

Finish A short finish with hints of forest floor and bark.

Texture Firm and plump.

• •

Jersey

6 Flavour **5** Saltiness **5** Sweetness **6** Umami

Nose Fresh shoreline and seaweed.

Body Crisp flavour of green wood and cucumber with a hint of lemon.

Finish A slow build up to a lingering tang of stainless steel.

Texture Thin and delicate.

• •

Lindisfarne

5 Flavour **5** Saltiness **5** Sweetness **5** Umami

Nose Generally neutral but with a very faint sense of sea-breeze.

Body Delicate butter with a distinct essence of melon coming through.

Finish A long clean metallic finish.

Texture Very silky.

• •

Maldon

6 Flavour **5** Saltiness **6** Sweetness **7** Umami

Nose Light aroma of the sea.

Body Rich flavour of walnut and avocado.

Finish Tart tang of steel followed by a sweet aftertaste.

Texture Smooth and meaty.

ROCK
Jersey

The pure island waters
bring a fresh seashore
and seaweed flavour with
a sapid, lingering, clean
finish to these plump,
quick-growing rock
oysters.

Rock oysters

Menai

6 Flavour **4** Saltiness **6** Sweetness **7** Umami

Nose Mild but defined astringent aroma of sea-salt.

Body Unmistakeable taste of grapefruit, apples and herbs.

Finish Two distinct flavours are apparent; copper and an earthy base reminiscent of a forest floor.

Texture Silky and meaty.

Poole

7 Flavour **4** Saltiness **4** Sweetness **6** Umami

Nose Light ozone.

Body Deep complex flavours of pecan nut, avocado and cucumber.

Finish Very short finish of musty pine. No aftertaste.

Texture Creamy, soft cheese.

Portland

6 Flavour **4** Saltiness **5** Sweetness **5** Umami

Nose Tangy brine.

Body A nutty butter flavour with hints of cucumber.

Finish A short syrupy finish with a noticeable earthiness.

Texture Plump and meaty.

River Exe

6 Flavour **5** Saltiness **7** Sweetness **7** Umami

Nose Natural bouquet of freshly-caught crab and pepper.

Body White sugar sweetness with suggestion of green sap and grass.

Finish Initial clean mineral hit followed by a lingering light mushroom essence.

Texture Very soft and silky.

R O C K
Menai

The fast-running waters of the Menai Straits bring an endless flow of nutrients to the oysters. Well fished, they have a fresh saline aroma with mineral and citrus character.

Rock oysters

River Teign

4 Flavour **3** Saltiness **7** Sweetness **5** Umami

Nose A very light freshwater nose.

Body Fills the mouth with refreshing cucumber and lettuce flavours.

Finish A sweet finish resembling watermelon.

Texture Crisp and juicy.

West Mersea

6 Flavour **7** Saltiness **5** Sweetness **5** Umami

Nose A clean, fresh faint nose of rockpools (iodine and seaweed).

Body Delicate cucumber and lettuce flavour.

Finish Long on the palate, earthy potting soil followed by a lingering tart metallic tang.

Texture Silky, delicate, plump.

Whitstable

6 Flavour **6** Saltiness **5** Sweetness **5** Umami

Nose A definite aroma of a sea breeze. Soft scent of seaweed and rockpools.

Body Mild taste of cut grass with hints of walnut shell and driftwood.

Finish A crisp metallic smack. Distinct tin with salt.

Texture Meaty and chewy.

ROCK
West Mersea

The islands and creeks
of the Colne Estuary
have some of the most-
renowned oysters of all.
Their sweet-saline flavour
of rockpools, iodine and
seaweed over minerals and
green vegetables is truly
distinctive.

OYSTER TYPES

Native oysters

• •

Colchester

9 Flavour   **3** Saltiness   **5** Sweetness   **8** Umami

Nose Strong salty nose.
Body Woody and herby, reminiscent of green sap.

Finish Big earthy flavours of mushroom, leather and bronze.
Texture Firm and meaty.

• •

English Channel

7 Flavour   **7** Saltiness   **4** Sweetness   **5** Umami

Nose Echoes of sea spray.
Body An intricate mix of walnut and driftwood with pear.

Finish Medium sweetness followed by a steel finish which departs quickly with no aftertaste.
Texture Plump and silky.

• •

Fal

4 Flavour   **4** Saltiness   **3** Sweetness   **5** Umami

Nose Iodine.
Body A juicy body with flavours of melon, lettuce and cucumber.

Finish A lingering light tin and copper finish.
Texture Firm and silky.

• •

Loch Ryan

5 Flavour   **7** Saltiness   **3** Sweetness   **4** Umami

Nose The smell of a sandy shore.
Body A nutty, woody oyster with lemon and cut grass overtones.

Finish A clean earthy zinc finish.
Texture Juicy and plump.

Loch Ryan

This ancient natural fishery
has beautifully-formed
natives with a vibrant ting
to the shells and juicy,
plump, firm meat with
a nutty, mineral, citrus,
chlorophyll taste.

OYSTER TYPES

Native oysters

Maldon

9 Flavour **6** Saltiness **4** Sweetness **5** Umami

Nose Brackish.
Body Very subtle taste of driftwood.

Finish A slow-burning strong metallic finish which builds to a crescendo.
Texture Chewy and firm.

Milford Haven

5 Flavour **3** Saltiness **3** Sweetness **3** Umami

Nose Salt and pepper.
Body Subtle walnut shell and wood.
Finish A long-lasting clean.

Texture Firm and plump.

Portsmouth Harbour

5 Flavour **9** Saltiness **3** Sweetness **8** Umami

Nose Iodine and saltwater.
Body A smooth salted butter and cucumber taste.

Finish A very clean, dry stainless steel finish.
Texture Meaty with just enough bite.

West Mersea

8 Flavour **8** Saltiness **5** Sweetness **5** Umami

Nose Very distinct briny nose.
Body A complex flavour – salted butter then sweet cashew.

Finish A lingering medium sweetness.
Texture Plump, firm and meaty.

Native oysters from Loch Ryan –
packed cup shell down shows the
beautiful blue tinge of the flat shell,
reflecting the colour of the Loch.

How to open a rock oyster

1. Hold the oyster cup shell-down firmly in a cloth on a solid board or work surface. Have the hinge towards you. Take the oyster knife and place at about two o'clock, taking the hinge at six o'clock.

2. Without using force, gently wriggle the knife at a 45 degree angle where the shells come together. The knife should begin to work between the shells, try moving the knife slightly back and fore.

3. When the shell 'gives', push the knife in further at an angle so it slides along the top shell, cutting through the adductor muscle. This will open the shell then it can be lifted with the knife and the top shell broken off at the hinge.

4. Turn the oyster with frill towards you and cut from right to left underneath the adductor muscle at the shell and flip the oyster over. Note: in France and many restaurants in the UK they do not turn the oyster, leaving it secured by the adductor muscle to be detached by the customer, usually with a flat oyster fork.

How to open a native oyster

1. A native oyster will fit cup shell down neatly into the palm. Place the frill into the base of the thumb, with the heel gripped by the fingers. Squeeze the oyster knife, flat side on, into the hinge. Carefully wriggle the knife back and forth until it cuts through the hinge. I strongly advise having a double cloth in the palm of the hand to grip the oyster and knife firmly.

2. When the hinge is broken, slide the knife along the inside of the top shell to cut through the adductor muscle. A little twist and lift will ensure the flesh of the oyster is not cut. Remove the top shell once the adductor muscle is completely cut.

3. Carefully remove traces of mud and shell, particularly from near the heel and frill. Retain all possible juice and gather any that spills.

4. Turn the oyster with frill towards you and cut from right to left underneath the adductor muscle at the shell and flip the oyster over to 'sunny side up'.

Choose your weapons

Over the centuries many items have been invented to open oysters. But all serious oyster houses will only use traditional oyster knives, usually opening rocks through the frill and natives through the hinge.

An American oyster opener usually uses a large heavy knife which is banged into the hinge with force parting the shells in one thrust. Many French ecaillers use a delicate technique, tickling the oyster from the side with a thin oyster knife. It is slipped in between the shells until the two ease apart revealing the succulent, delicate mollusc inside.

Remember do not thrust, just tickle and they will part easily.

1. The classic knife is the perfect present for an oyster lover (from Wright Bros).

2. My traditional knife with a rounded end.

3. Everyday, inexpensive oyster knife from Wright Bros.

4. Everyday French knife with useful guard.

5. Solid sharp-tipped knife, perfect for natives.

Dress them up!

Oyster purists will eat them with just their natural juice, and they are truly delicious. However they are receptive to flavours that slightly enliven them. Try a squeeze of fresh lemon juice, some plain vinegar, or as the French enjoy them with shallot vinegar. This is simply finely diced fresh shallots with good wine vinegar; if you can get them the 'eschalotes grises' or Bordeaux shallots are the finest.

Spice up oysters with a twist of black pepper, plain white pepper, cayenne or paprika. Tabasco sauce, made from vinegar and red chilli peppers, aged in barrels, has long been a great favourite. Whatever the preference, it is always fun to dress up a few to suit your mood!

1. Tabasco
2. Lemon
3. Cayenne pepper
4. Black pepper
5. White wine shallot vinegar

RECIPE

Oyster grilled with herb butter

This simple dish can cover a wide range of flavours according to the herbs used. It's a dish to vary according to the season and availability of fresh herbs. Garlic, shallots and peppers can be added according to taste.

RECIPE

Oyster grilled with herb butter

Ingredients

24 rock oysters opened on half shell

100g unsalted butter softened

25ml extra virgin olive oil

4 dessertspoons finely chopped fresh herbs: parsley, coriander, dill, fennel, basil, chives, mint etc

1 dessertspoon lemon juice

Good twist of black pepper, and a pinch of cayenne pepper

Method

Have a grill tray large enough to take the oysters and two sheets of baking foil crumpled on the bottom to hold the oysters level. Heat the grill to full.

Make a selection of herbs of your choice and chop finely then immediately mix into the butter with a fork or spatula, working in the olive oil and lemon juice.

Loosen the oysters from the shell reserving as much juice as possible and arrange on a roasting tray covered with lightly crumpled foil. Put a level teaspoonful of the herb butter onto each oyster, top up the juice in the shells and put under the grill for 2 – 3 minutes until the butter is just sizzling golden brown and the oysters are just heated through.

Put onto deep serving plates and have plenty of bread to soak up the juices.

Tasting notes

The herb combination, ideally from freshly picked herbs from the garden, will help bring out the elusive vegetal and herb notes in oysters. The flavours of cucumber, avocado, lettuce, geranium, melon, lemon, grass, sap, iodine, cashew, walnut, butter, seaweed, driftwood, copper, zinc, steel, earth, mushroom and cream all come from the oyster tasters' vocabulary. This simple herb, butter, oil and spice combination eases up these natural flavours to complement taste images experienced.

RECIPE

Oyster with spinach and bacon

These plump and juicy Loch Ryan Natives have the savour of nuts, wood, lemon and grass complemented with the firm mineral flavours of the overcoat spinach that keeps the oyster succulent and flavoursome.

RECIPE

Oyster with spinach and bacon

Ingredients

24 oysters (rock or native), opened on the half shell

50g thinly sliced un-smoked dry cured streaky bacon without rind. Or use your favourite charcuterie such Parma ham, Serrano ham, Bayonne ham, or thinly sliced chorizo, salchichon, or salami.

10ml vegetable oil

50g shallots, finely chopped

250g spinach leaves

2 dessertspoons chopped fresh herbs: parsley, coriander, dill, fennel, etc

100g soft cream cheese

1 dessertspoon lemon juice

Good twist of black pepper, a pinch of white and cayenne pepper, and a touch of grated nutmeg

Method

Have a grill tray large enough to take the oysters and two sheets of baking foil crumpled on the bottom to hold the oysters level. Heat the grill to full.

Fry the bacon, ham or salami in oil until just crisp, then remove. Add shallots to the pan and cook until softening. Chop the spinach into 2cm pieces approximately, and add to the pan, stir and cover to allow it to wilt. Add the cream cheese and stir well seasoning with pepper, nutmeg and lemon juice. Cook gently until just soft.

Snip a few slivers of bacon over each oyster and top each with the spinach mixture just to cover. Place under the grill to cook for 2 – 3 minutes until sizzling and beginning to turn slightly golden. The oysters will be just warm through beneath.

Tasting notes

Serve with Chablis or Manzanilla. Popeye's favourite way with oysters brings the mineral nuances of the oysters with the most distinctive vegetal flavour. The two savours elevate each other into this powerful, invigorating dish that will liven taste buds hitherto unknown. The steely dryness of the Chablis or the sea smack calcareous nature of the Manzanilla will elevate the minerality further.

RECIPE

Oyster with blue cheese and laverbread

The Welsh speciality laverbread is from the same seaweed used for *nori* in Japan. The fresh seaweed grows on the intertidal zone. It has a deep mineral iodine taste and is the most palatable of all edible seaweeds. The combination with oysters is so natural, as they grow in the same area. Often oyster trestles and perches are covered with a natural growth of laver. The light cheese topping gives a vibrant sizzle to the dish.

RECIPE

Oyster with blue cheese and laverbread

Ingredients

24 rock oysters, opened on half shell

100g laverbread

100g blue cheese such as a mild Stilton, Bath blue, Cornish blue, or Perl Las

100g low fat curd cheese

10ml white wine or cider vinegar

Tabasco sauce

Method

Have a grill tray large enough to take the oysters and two sheets of baking foil. Heat the grill to full. Loosen the oysters from the shell and reserve the juices.

Mix 10ml of the juice with the vinegar and mix into the laverbread, add a good dash Tabasco.

Mash the blue cheese and curd cheese together mixing in 10ml oyster juice.

Lift each oyster from the shell and place a scant teaspoon of laverbread into the cup shell. Replace the oyster and top with a flat teaspoon of the cheese mixture.

Take a grill or roasting tray, lightly crumple sheets of foil and place into the bottom of the tray. Arrange the oysters onto the foil so they do not tip. Sprinkle the remaining oyster juice into the shells, put under the grill and cook for a few minutes until they are sizzling on top and lightly golden.

Transfer the oysters onto a large serving platter or individual plates of six.

Serve with La Gitana Manzanilla, lightly chilled.

Tasting notes

The Manzanilla has the taste of the sea spray, while the oysters and seaweed are from the sea bed. The fast tides over the oyster beds brings the nutrients that give their mineral flavour, just as the chalk soil gives Manzanilla its dry calcareous taste. Both marry well as they are complete in their own flavours. The vegetal smack of the seaweed and the creaminess of the cheese reflect both ranges of the taste experience from the glorious oyster: the nuances of the low tide and the subtle creamy flavour with its nutty and cornfield autumn aromas.

RECIPE

Oyster crisp-fried in breadcrumbs

This might be 'doing a scampi' with the glorious oyster bringing it to an ignominious end – but the crunch of the crisp crumbs and the succulence of the mollusc contained inside is an incredible combination. Pan-fried, not deep-fried, the oyster retains its taste and texture deliciously. I have introduced newcomers to oysters with this dish. The method was originally from Robert Carrier and the crumb coating from Union Square Café, New York.

RECIPE

Oyster crisp-fried in breadcrumbs

Ingredients

24 oysters (rock or native), opened on the half shell

100g organic plain flour, or gram flour, sifted

3 eggs beaten until smooth

15 wholemeal cheese crackers, ground into fine crumbs

25ml vegetable oil

25g butter

1 dessertspoon chopped fresh herbs: parsley, coriander

1 dessertspoon chopped capers

100g mayonnaise

1 dessertspoon lemon juice

Good twist of black pepper

a pinch of white and cayenne pepper

One lemon, quartered

Method

Remove the oysters from the shells. Drain the juice and reserve half, add the rest to the egg and beat in well. Put the shells in a low oven or under a low grill to warm through.

Have three bowls with flour, egg and biscuit crumbs in a line.

Add a pinch of peppers to the flour. Dust the oysters in the flour, then dip into the egg and then the crumbs to coat lightly and arrange on a board. When all oysters are ready, melt the oil and butter in a large pan until bubbling but not burning. Place each oyster into the pan (you might do this in batches) and cook for about 30 seconds or until just golden, turn over and cook on the other side. Lift out and put each oyster in a shell.

Meantime add some or all of the remaining oyster juice to the mayonnaise to dilute slightly, add the herbs and capers and mix well.

Serve oysters on plates with a bowl of the sauce and a quarter of lemon.

Tasting notes

This dish will overcome any misguided notions of the frightening texture of oysters. The crunch of the cracker crumbs has the ring of fried scampi or chicken nuggets, yet the succulent sea smack savour sings of the natural minerals and the subtle flavours of mushroom, avocado, cucumber, pecan, walnut, leather, bronze, zinc and all the wonderful nuances that these remarkable molluscs contain.

The sizzling buttery crunch and the calcareous savour inside direct me straight to a Chablis that has the buttery notes of chardonnay with the mineral backbone of the chalky limestone soil of the area.

RECIPE

Oyster with fried garlic, sesame and coriander

This recipe is a flavour combination with familiar Eastern ingredients: garlic, sesame and herbs. These provide taste and texture contrasts that allow the very lightly cooked – indeed first frightened – oyster to shine through.

RECIPE

Oysters with fried garlic, sesame and coriander

Ingredients

24 rock oysters, opened on half shell

4 plump garlic cloves

10ml vegetable oil

25ml sesame oil

4 dessertspoons finely chopped parsley or coriander

1 lemon

Method

Have a grill tray large enough to take the oysters and two sheets of crumpled baking foil. Heat the grill to full.

Loosen the oysters in the shell, reserving as much juice as possible, and arrange on a roasting tray covered with lightly crumpled foil. Put a dash of sesame onto each oyster and place under the grill for 1 – 2 minutes.

Meanwhile thinly slice the garlic cloves and fry gently in a pan with the vegetable oil until light golden and just crisp. Remove oysters from the grill and spoon several garlic crisps onto each oyster.

Put the remaining sesame oil and lemon juice into the warm pan and just heat through. Add half the parsley or coriander then spoon a dribble over each oyster. Put under the grill for a few seconds; do not allow the garlic to colour further. Arrange onto serving plates and top with remaining parsley or coriander. Cut the remaining lemon into four and serve with the oysters, with Tabasco sauce and a little more sesame oil.

Tasting notes

Serve with a glass of Taittinger Champagne – the tiny bubbles explode on the palate with the warm fresh sea savour of the oysters. The herby tang and biscuity aromatic crunch of the garlic brings out the yeasty zestiness of the champagne. The texture of the crisp garlic cuts the smooth richness of the oyster, while the herbs tease the green grape taste and the rich toasted oil rounds the depth of the complex champagne.

Oyster with chilli and celery crumbs

The coolness of celery and heat of the chilli make this a vibrant dish that brings out all of the flavour of the oyster, yet amazingly does not overpower.

RECIPE

Oyster with chilli and celery crumbs

Ingredients

24 oysters (rock or native), opened on the half shell

20ml vegetable oil

50g shallots finely chopped

2 plump green chillies, de-seeded and chopped finely

1 dessertspoon each finely chopped fresh celery leaves and parsley (or coriander)

Six wholemeal crackers, ground to crumbs

25ml extra virgin olive oil

1 lemon

Method

Have a grill tray large enough to take the oysters and two sheets of baking foil, crumpled on the bottom to hold the oysters level. Heat the grill to full.

Place oysters on the grill tray with all their juice for 2 – 3 minutes maximum.

Fry the shallots in a pan with the vegetable oil until slightly golden.

Add the chillies, celery leaves and parsley, and cook quickly until colouring slightly. Add half the crumbs to soak up the juice and mix with shallot and chilli. Spoon a little over each oyster using all then dust with the remaining crumbs and put back under the grill for a few seconds, taking care the crumbs do not burn.

Arrange on plates, top each with a drizzle of best olive oil and serve with a wedge of lemon, a good twist of black pepper, and a pinch of white and Tabasco sauce.

Tasting notes

The heat of the chilli subtly drenched over the oyster makes a flavour contrast that demonstrates oysters, as other molluscs, can take spices well. Yet the sweetness of the oyster shines through with cucumber, cashew and copper, building to a crescendo with the zippy taste of the chilli.

The wine for this is a fresh clean Muscadet that has the balance of lemon and fruit, elevating the sweetness of the oyster and acting as a cooler for the chilli. As each oyster is enjoyed with an alternate tipple of Muscadet the flavour of each builds up, making this a dish that should not come to an end.

Oyster festivals

Oysters have been a major part of the livelihood in many coastal areas where oyster beds have flourished since Roman times. Hence the oyster has been celebrated in many oyster festivals that take place, usually to mark the start of the oyster season in September.

One of the oldest oyster festivals is the grand ceremony run by Colchester Council that takes place in the medieval Moot Hall in Colchester. It's a terribly grand affair with a splendid procession and banquet luncheon starting with Colchester native oysters followed by much other local seafood. I have been a guest at this fine occasion.

Perhaps the best known of all is the Galway Oyster Festival which celebrates the wonderful oysters of Galway Bay, and in true Irish style the celebration and hospitality continues all weekend. Copious quantities of Guinness are consumed as imbibers enjoy oysters by the dozen.
The entertainment is legendary.

The Anglesey Oyster Festival takes place at the start of October and the fine oysters of the Menai are celebrated in numerous pubs and restaurants throughout the island. There are special menus and entertainment throughout the weekend.

The Falmouth Oyster Festival takes place in the summer and celebrates the only remaining fishery that relies on sail power to pull the dredges. It also notes the fine array of native and rock oysters that come from the various creeks and rivers. Frenchman's Creek, Helford River Natives and River Fal oysters make up the copious supply. It is also the time of the year to enjoy the full bounty of the Cornish seas with crab, lobster, bass and mackerel in their full season.

The Whitstable Oyster Festival celebrates the Royal Charter of the fine natives in an area that has become one of the top destinations for oyster and seafood lovers.

The North East Oyster Festival is a weekend of oysters and local fare in County Durham.

June

Colchester Medieval and Oyster Fayre
Colchester, Essex
www.oysterfayre.co.uk

Rock Oyster Festival
Wadebridge, Cornwall
www.rockoysterfestival.co.uk

July

The Whitstable Oyster Festival
Whitstable, Kent
www.whitstableoysterfestival.com

September

Galway Oyster Festival
Galway, Ireland
www.galwayoysterfest.com

North East Oyster Festival
Hardwick Hall Hotel, Sedgefield,
County Durham
www.theoysterfestival.co.uk

Woburn Oyster Festival
Woburn, Bedforshire
www.woburnoysterfestival.co.uk

October

Anglesey Oyster and Welsh Produce Festival
Trearddur Bay Hotel,
Trearddur Bay, Anglesey
www.tentopanglesey.co.uk

Falmouth Oyster Festival
Falmouth, Cornwall
www.falmouthoysterfestival.co.uk

The Colchester Oyster Festival
Moot Hall, Colchester

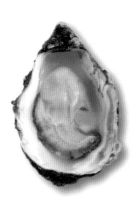

London Oyster Guide 🦪

CHARLES CAMPION

Days out from London

There's nothing, quite nothing, so much fun as a good skive.

This invaluable guide gives the oyster lover plenty of scope for adventure within the boundary of the M25, but what about those occasions when you would really benefit from a day (and possibly even a night) in the country? This is my personal selection of places where you can tuck into some decent oysters while playing truant from London, and some of Colin's favourites in Wales.

Charles Campion

---

1. Café Royal Oyster Bar, Edinburgh

19 West Register Street, Edinburgh, EH2 2AA **0131 556 1884**
www.caferoyal.org.uk

The baroque splendour of this fine Edwardian institution remains the favourite of oyster aficionados. You might see many notables tucking into a dozen number twos while sipping a glass of Chablis. Oysters natural, Rockefeller and Kilpatrick, Scottish beef and ale pie, and Café Royal fish stew are among the reasonably priced hearty dishes.

---

2. English's, Brighton

29 – 31 East Street, Brighton, East Sussex, BN1 1HL **01273 327980**
www.englishs.co.uk

This utterly traditional English restaurant remains true to fine ingredients and impeccable service. The fare includes Dover sole, halibut, turbot, bass, crab, lobster, mussels and wonderful oysters. You might get a space at the oyster bar, find a table inside or on the al fresco area at the start of the famous Brighton lanes.

---

3. Hix Oyster and Fish House, Lyme Regis

Cobb Road, Lyme Regis, Dorset, DT7 3JP
01297 446910
www.hixoysterandfishhouse.co.uk

The fabulous location overlooks Lyme Bay where fishing boats bob on the open sea. It's the setting for some of the best from the sea cooked in true modern British style. Oysters come from local producers in Dorset, Devon and Cornwall as well as perhaps West Mersea, Cumbrae and Loch Ryan.

Hix Oyster and Fish House
Lyme Regis, Dorset.

4. La Braseria, Swansea

28 Wind Street, Swansea, SA1 1DZ
01792 469683
www.labraseria.com

Fresh oysters are part of the offer in the bountiful display of fresh fish and meats, set in display counters in the large restaurant complex. All can be enjoyed in the bustling ambience, or a platter of rock oysters can be taken in the smaller and more intimate La Prensa bar that adjoins the main restaurant.

5. La Marina, Penarth

The Old Custom House, Penarth,
Cardiff, CF64 1TT **029 2070 5544**
www.theoldcustomhousepenarth.co.uk

Close to the capital's centre and bustling Cardiff Bay, this large restaurant empire has spacious dining on two floors. Fresh seafood groans in an ice-filled counter and includes bass, monkfish, Dover sole, sewin in season, crab, lobster, prawns, mussels and large rock oysters. A selection of finest meats all cooked on 'la parilla' completes the copious selection together with a fabulous wine cellar.

6. Oyster Shack, Bigbury Devon

Milburn Orchard Farm, Stakes Hill, Bigbury, Devon, TQ7 4BE **01548 810876**
www.oystershack.co.uk

Timing is everything while planning your platter of local rock oysters here, for the sea covers the road at high tide. This makes it obligatory for a second platter as seafood lovers await the ebb tide. Oysters come au naturel or perhaps grilled with chorizo, with garlic butter or bacon. Fresh crab, lobster, moules, prawns and calamari make up the seafood lover's dream.

7. Rogano

11 Exchange Place, Glasgow, G1 3AN
0141 248 4055
www.roganoglasgow.com

This legendary Glasgow institution with its art deco design has been serving oysters and seafood specialities for seventy-five years. The cuisine extends from freshest oysters and many cooked dishes to lobster, crab and international styles including paella, sushi and superb meat and game from the Highlands.

8. The Company Shed, West Mersea Island

129 Coast Road, West Mersea, Colchester, Essex, CO5 8PA **01206 382700**
www.the-company-shed.co.uk

It's well worth the trip from London to enjoy some of the freshest seafood at amazing prices at this unpretentious place, as the name sounds, run by the Haward oyster family. Having tended the beds of the Colne and West Mersea for generations, they proffer the finest natives from Mersea with their plump sweet flesh and delicious rocks from the same beds.

9. The Ferryboat Inn, Helford

Helford Passage, Falmouth, Cornwall, TR11 5LB **01326 250625**
www.ferryboatinnhelford.com

The idyllic setting on the Helford River is just down river from the famous Duchy of Cornwall oyster beds, and Frenchman's Creek, the inspiration for Daphne du Maurier's novel. Expect the freshest seafood from boats of the region and wonderful oysters with the aroma of the sea lapping the shore. Eat al fresco in summer and by log fires in the winter at this all-year-round destination.

10. The Harbourmaster, Aberaeron

Pen Cei, Aberaeron, Ceredigion, SA46 0BT
01545 570755
www.harbour-master.com

You can smell the briny smack of the high tide, and the seaweed savour of the low tide in the harbour when you dine in this boutique quayside brasserie and restaurant. The fare includes much from local boats: crab, lobster, prawns, bass, mackerel, and oysters from over the waters of the Irish Sea from Carlingford Lough.

11. The Lobster Pot, Church Bay, Anglesey

Church Bay, Nr Holyhead,
Anglesey, LL65 4EU **01407 730241**
www.lobster-pot.net

This place unfazed by time started serving lobster teas from the lobster ponds next door in the 1950s. The seafood comes from local boats collected fresh daily; oysters and fine mussels come from the Menai Straits at Brynsiencyn, close to where Halen Mon Anglesey sea salt is harvested. It's wonderfully unpretentious with correct cooking, prices and bargain wines.

12. Whitstable Oyster Company

Royal Native Oyster Stores, Horsebridge,
Whitstable, Kent, CT5 1BU
01227 276856
www.whitstableoystercompany.com

Overlooking the Thames estuary this considerable operation all started in a small hut. Oysters come direct from the famous beds with a Royal Charter, and these include the fine native (in season) and rock oysters that start in their own hatchery. A wide range of fish, much of it local, comes in great straightforward dishes.

The Ferryboat Inn, Helford.

Merchants and suppliers

London

Billingsgate Market

Trafalgar Way, Poplar, E14 5ST

Bards Shellfish, contact Simon or Ben Chilcott, Stands H6, H7, H8, H9, H10. tel 0207 538 2835 bardshell@yahoo.co.uk

A. A. Lyons, contact Tony Lyons, Stands 11, 12, 13, 14, 15. tel 0207 537 3263 lyonscharlotte@hotmail.com

Micks Eel Supply, contact Mick or Joe Jenrick, shop 18. tel 020 7515 2249

R&G Shellfish, contact Ray Brand, stand G5, shop 2+3. tel 0207 515 9419, 01708 472 092

John Stockwell, contact Eddie or Steve Monahan, shop 13+14. tel 0207 987 7776

T. Bush, contact Bob or Joe Suett, stand D7. tel 0207 515 1345

Maldon Oyster Company Ltd
Birchwood Farm, Cock Clarks, Chelmsford, Essex, CM3 6RF
01621 828699
www.maldonoyster.com

Rossmore Oysters Ltd
Lakeview, Old Hollow, Worth, Sussex, RH10 4TA
01293 888868
sales@oysters.co.uk
www.oysters.co.uk

Richard Haward's Oysters
129 Coast Road, West Mersea, Colchester, Essex, CO5 8PA
01206 383284
enquiries@richardhawardsoysters.co.uk
www.richardhawardsoysters.co.uk

Wright Brothers Ltd
9 Park Street, Borough Market, SE1 9AB
020 7403 9559
info@wrightbrothers.com
www.thewrightbrothers.co.uk

Outside London

Bigbury Bay Oysters
Milburn Orchard, Stakes Hill, Bigbury, Devon, TQ7 4BE
01548 811130
mail@bigburybayoysters.co.uk
www.bigburybayoysters.co.uk

Camel Oysters
Stakes Hill, Porthhilly, Rock nr Wadebridge, Cornwall
porthhillyfarm@aol.com

The Caledonian Oyster Co Ltd
01631 570222
www.caledonianoyster.co.uk

Carlingford Lough Oyster Company Ltd
Mullatee, Carlingford, Co Louth, Ireland
00353 429373800
www.carlingfordoysterco.ie

Colchester Oyster Fishery
Pyefleet Quay, Mersea Island,
Colchester, Essex, CO5 8UN
01206 384141
info@colchesteroysterfishery.com
www.colchesteroysterfishery.com

Colonsay
Isle of Colonsay Oysters,
01951 200365

Cornish Native Oysters
Admiralty Quay, Mylor Harbour,
Falmouth, Cornwall, TR11 5UF
07791 378503
contacts@cornishnativeoysters.co.uk
www.cornishnativeoysters.co.uk

Cumbrae Oysters Ltd
07977 043710
info@cumbraeoysters.com
www.cumbraeoysters.com

Dorset Oyster Ltd
13 Benson Road, Nuffield Trading
Estate, Poole, Dorset, BH13 0GB
01202 666057
pete@dorsetoysters.com
www.dorsetoysters.com

Duchy Oyster Farm, Wright Brothers
Port Navas, Falmouth,
Cornwall, TR11 5RJ
01326 340210
info@duchyoysterfarm.com
www.duchyoysterfarm.com

Guernsey Oysters
Raymond Falla House, Longue Rue,
St Martin, Guernsey, GY1 6AF
01481 234567

The Jersey Oyster Company
La Ferme, La Rue de la Sente
Maillard, Grouville, Jersey, JE3 9FE
01534 852553
info@jerseyoyster.com
www.jerseyoyster.com

Lindisfarne Oysters
West House, Ross Farm, Belford,
Northumberland, NE70 7EN
01668 213870
enquiry@lindisfarneoysters.co.uk
www.lindisfarneoysters.co.uk

Loch Fyne Oysters Ltd
Clachan, Cairndow, Argyll,
Scotland, PA26 8BL
01499 600470
info@lochfyne.com
www.lochfyne.com

**Loch Ryan Oyster Fishery
Company Ltd**
c/o Rossmore Oysters Ltd,
Lakeview, Old Hollow, Worth,
Sussex, RH10 4TA
01293 888868
sales@oysters.co.uk
www.oysters.co.uk

Menai Oysters
Tal-y-Bont Bach, Dwyran,
Llanfairpwll, Anglesey, LL61 6UU
01248 430878
www.menaioysters.co.uk

Othniel Oysters Ltd
Fax 01202 710683
www.othniel.com

Merchants and suppliers

Portland Oysters
Ferrymans Way, Portland Road,
Wyke Regis, Dorset, DT4 9YU
01305 788867
info@crabhousecafe.co.uk
www.crabhousecafe.co.uk

River Exe Oysters
Oak Farm, Kenton,
Nr Exeter, Devon, EX6 8EZ
01626 890133
david@shellfish.org.uk

River Teign Shellfish
10 Lower Brookfield,
Lustleigh, Newton Abbot,
Devon, TQ13 9TP
01647 277476
riverteignshellfish1@hotmail.com

The Whitstable Shellfish Company
Westmeads Road, Whitstable,
Kent, CT5 1LW
01227 361199
sales@whitstable-shellfish.co.uk

www.cornishnativeoysters.co.uk

Markets and retailers

Borough Market
8 Southwark Street, Southwark,
London, SE1 1TL
020 7407 1002
www.boroughmarket.org.uk
Thursday – Saturday
Richard Haward's Oysters
⊖ London Bridge

Marylebone Farmers Market
Cramer Street Car Park, Marylebone,
London, W1U 4EW
Sunday 9 – 2pm
Maldon Oysters
⊖ Regent's Park

Partridges Food Market
Duke of York Square Market,
Kings Road, Chelsea,
London, SW3 4LY
www.partridges.co.uk/foodmarket
Saturday 10 – 4pm
Maldon Oysters
⊖ Sloane Square

Pimlico Farmers Market
Orange Square, Corner of Pimlico
Road and Ebury Street, Pimlico,
London, SW1W 8UT
Saturday 9 –1pm
⊖ Sloane Square

Also oysters may be sold in season
at other London Markets.
www.lfm.org.uk

Waitrose
www.waitrose.com
Most Waitrose supermarket that
have a fish counter with oysters.

Waitrose Belgravia
27 Motcomb Street, Belgravia,
London, SW1X 8GG
020 7235 4958
⊖ Hyde Park Corner

John Lewis Food Hall
300 Oxford Street, London, W1A 1EX
020 7629 7711
⊖ Oxford Circus

Waitrose Kings Road
196 Kings Road, Chelsea,
London, SW3 5XP
020 7351 2775
⊖ Sloane Square

Waitrose Marylebone
98 – 101 Marylebone High Street,
London, W1U 4SD
020 7935 4787
⊖ Regent's Park

Harrods Food Hall
87 –135 Brompton Road,
Knightsbridge, London, SW1X 7XL
020 7730 1234
⊖ Knightsbridge

Selfridges Food Hall
James Knight Fishmongers,
400 Oxford Street,
London, W1A 1AB
020 7318 3725
⊖ Bond Street

Fortnum and Mason
181 Piccadilly,
London, W1A 1ER
020 7734 8040
⊖ Piccadilly Circus

GENERAL

Index

INDEX

Restaurants A – L

London Oyster Guide

INDEX

Restaurants L – Z

INDEX
Merchants and suppliers

Mature native oysters are harvested at
4-5 years old and rock oysters at $2\frac{1}{2}$-3 years
old depending on location.

THE AUTHOR

Colin Pressdee

Colin Pressdee was brought up in the village of Oystermouth in Mumbles, an oyster fishing village dating back to Roman times. As a child he remembers the remains of oyster smacks on the shores, and the oyster perches where the boats used to deposit their oysters. He opened the Oyster Perches restaurant, followed by the Drangway, in Swansea. These specialised in seafood and oysters from fisheries including Colchester and Cornwall. Now a food writer and consultant living in London he retains close links with Wales. He has always promoted oysters and seafood with many clients and friends. He has been a long time member of the Shellfish Association of Great Britain. He has written several books on seasonal food and the countryside. '*Food Wales – a second helping*' is regarded as an authoritative guide to seasonality of food. '*Food Wales eating out guide*' is the most comprehensive listing of where to eat in Wales. As a lifelong oyster enthusiast, he knows numerous places in London where oysters are available.

www.colinpressdee.com

RESEARCHER

Carwyn Evans

Carwyn Evans been involved in the catering industry since his college days. Now he works on consultancy projects with Colin and has undertaken work all over Europe, the UK and as far as Yemen on projects with the British Council promoting British food. He has done the research and development for all the *Food Wales* books. Now with the *London Oyster Guide*, he has searched out over 150 restaurants, pubs and bars serving oysters, plus the markets, retail and festivals selling and promoting oysters, and the merchants in London and producers around the coast. He is a travel enthusiast which inevitably involves searching out oysters in numerous destinations around the World.

me the SAGB has steadily extended

Shellfish
Association of Great Britain

The Shellfish Association of Great Britain, or SAGB, is the trade association for the UK shellfish industry. Our membership is composed of shellfish catchers and harvesters, farmers, commercial traders, managers, scientists and restaurateurs.

First founded as the Oyster Merchants' and Planters' Association in 1903, and renamed the Shellfish Association of Great Britain in 1969, the SAGB has steadily extended its range of activities from 'harvest to sale' in over a century of support to the industry. Our aim is to assist and promote the sustainable development of the Shellfish Industry in the United Kingdom from 'sea to plate'.

The SAGB represents the interests and views of the whole shellfish supply chain in a number of vital areas, for example the development and enforcement of legislation affecting the growing, harvesting and marketing of shellfish, and the refinement of policies affecting all of these areas. The SAGB is recognised as 'the voice of UK shellfish' by many people and organisations.

The SAGB is the promoter of shellfish in the UK. As well as producing recipe booklets we have

published a detailed report covering the nutritional value of shellfish with data that has been used to develop species-specific nutritional factsheets and a pamphlet that debunks the 'old-wives tale' that eating prawns raises your cholesterol levels.

We have also produced a series of 'how to' films for shellfish preparation and cooking. These can be viewed on our YouTube site www.youtube.com/ShellfishGB

Join the SAGB today – you will become part of, and support, a strong body that works to help you.

See our website for more details www.shellfish.org.uk or follow us on Twitter @SAGB

Credits

Published by Graffeg
Copyright © Graffeg 2011
ISBN 978 1 905582563

Graffeg,
Radnor Court,
256 Cowbridge Road East,
Cardiff CF5 1GZ Wales UK.
T: +44 (0)29 2078 5156
sales@graffeg.com
www.graffeg.com

Designed and produced by
Peter Gill & Associates
sales@petergill.com
www.petergill.com

A CIP Catalogue record for this book
is available from the British Library.

Graffeg are hereby identified as the
authors of this work in accordance
with section 77 of the Copyrights,
Designs and Patents Act 1988.

Map base information reproduced by
permission of Ordnance Survey on
behalf of HMSO. © Crown Copyright
(2011). All rights reserved. Ordnance
Survey Licence number 100020518.

London Oyster Guide written by
Colin Pressdee and Carwyn Evans.

Every effort has been made to
ensure that the information in this
book is current and it is given in
good faith at the time of publication.
Please be aware that circumstances
can change and be sure to check
details before visiting any of the
restaurants featured.

Images;
© Philboormanphotography;
Front cover, IFC, 7, 9, 11, 13, 15,
17-19, 85, 87, 89, 91, 93, 95, 97-105,
107-109, 111-113, 115-117, 119-121,
123-125, 127, IBC, back cover.
© Dominick Tyler 4. © Colin
Pressdee 6. © Cubbit House 29,
back cover. © Racine 39. © ETM
Group 47, 56. © Caprice Holdings
55. © Le Vacherin 65. © Shellfish
Association of Great Britain; Sylvette
Peplowski 67, 79, 81, 141, 143;
David Jarrad 141. © Hix 131.
© The Wright Brothers 133.
© Cornishnativeoysters.co.uk;
Mike Thomas 136, back cover.

For information, news, events,
phone and tablet apps visit
londonoysterguide.com